Taxing Economic Rents

How to tax economic rents
and
why your economic survival
depends on introducing the
economic rent tax

BY

TIM WALSHAW

ISBN: 978-0-9876113-0-7

Previous related publication by Tim Walshaw:
Increasing Returns to Scale: A Simple Way to Make Good Investments, and Not Bad Investments, When Investing in Company Shares. **Published 2014.**
Economic Rents, the Hidden Profit: How to Find Safe Companies to Invest In. **Published 2015.**

\<publisher Tim Walshaw\>
\<Canberra, Australia\>

\<2016\>

Contents

Preface

Everybody hates taxes. Everybody hates talking about taxes. Yet tax is one of the most pervasive influences in civilized human experience. Next to war, taxes and the other side of the coin (no pun intended) government expenditure, have the biggest influences on not only society's structure and behavior, but also everything else up to including the level of human happiness. Taxation has been the leitmotiv of all human history back to the stone ages. The way taxation has been handled by the rulers through the ages has been the ultimate cause of the rise and fall of all civilisations. Too much taxation has destroyed countries, empires and civilisations. Badly designed taxes have led to revolts, civil wars, bloodshed, defeat in wars. To say that the subject of taxation is vital is a massive understatement. The subject of taxation, next to perhaps sex and security, is, if you really think about it, at the absolute core of any society's continued existence.

Yet taxation has always treated in a haphazard manner. "Suck it and see" has been the standard methodology of rulers through the ages, from pharaohs, emperors, kings and parliaments.

The approach goes something like this. There is a need. So "we try this tax". Sometimes it works. Sometimes it doesn't. If for some accidental reason it works and the imposition of this tax does not cause too much harm, economically or socially, or worse causes a violent reaction from the populace, the tax becomes ingrained and traditional until conditions change and this tax ceases to raise sufficient revenue. Then there is a crisis, and a new arbitrary tax is tried.

I

Along with this theme, there is always constant pressure by certain sections of society to transfer the burden of tax on other sections of society, usually less powerful and influential. Sometimes this works, if only for a time. But frequently there is a push back, and the government finds to its pain that this tax transfer was a mistake.

This process has been going on for time immemorial. The purpose of this book is, for the first time ever (yes ever, never in the history of the human race has this been attempted), to break governments and society out of this horrible cycle.

True, this book is not designed to prevent governments spending too much. That subject will be relegated to a later book on the "maximum level of government expenditure". (Yes, such an estimation is possible – just count the level and expense of supporting non-producers – there is theoretically a "tipping point"). However before that disastrous level is reached, inefficient taxes will massively reduce the growth and indeed the level of the economy. Inefficient taxes themselves carry a hidden tax, called by economists the "excess burden", that consumes a greater and greater proportion of the economy as the tax rate rises, and does not return this tax to the economy. Thus the inefficient and rapacious government is doomed much sooner than it expects.

As will be shown later in this book, the maximum possible proportion of taxes to GDP in the economy is around sixty per cent, before the economy collapses. As the proportion of taxes in the economy of most nations has been rising steadily in the post war period, it can be shown that regardless how advanced those countries are, regardless of what these countries spend their taxes on, the tax system will rapidly (at a rate of change equal to the square of the tax rate) doom those countries as the tax level rises.

The only way out of this immediate predicament is an immediate switch to taxes on economic rents, replacing ALL taxes.

Why has this not occurred to date? The major reason is that there has been a general belief that economic rents are "generally too low" and not worth taxing, except for mineral extraction. This belief stems from the incorrect assumption that all economic rents stem from monopoly rents, so competition will reduce most economic rents in the general economy. There is also the related Marxist belief which influences many economists that monopoly rents are declining and will eventually disappear.

In fact the major source of economic rents have nothing to do with monopolies, oligopolies or the level of competition, but are due to "market imperfections". As you will see from the list of market imperfection given later in this book, most have nothing to do with the level of competition. In other words, even under a system of pure competition (that economic ideal) economic rents would continue to exist. Firms would continue to generate economic rents even under conditions of intense competition. There will be always high and sustained economic rents. And they can be taxed.

Introduction

The purpose of this book is to explain the nature of, and the benefits of, a tax on economic rents. It will go through the theoretical background of taxes on economic rents, which can be divided into taxes on business income and employment income, and a subgroup of taxes on land values. The book will then describe why these economic rents taxes are theoretically efficient. Finally the book will describe the major benefits to be gained from this economic efficiency, and compare these benefits with the losses incurred by the present system. Finally the book will ground these losses and their effects onto something everybody understand and fears – unemployment.

The arrangement of this book is in the form of a simplified economic argument and analysis. There will be many who will see all the diagrams and their eyes will glaze. There will be a few who would argue that there should be a lot more mathematics and proofs! I have chosen the bare minimum level of economic argument understandable to a well-educated non-economist. There is one mathematical proof, otherwise I have referred to more mathematical approaches in the references. Furthermore I have chosen an economic argument rather than the usual bombastic case put in by accountants, lawyers and lobbyists "I want this, I don't want that" as I am aiming for a tax structure that benefits all, not just for those who write submissions and try to influence government.

Reasons for tax increases

Over the years governments have increased taxes for just two reasons:
1. Governments are under pressure, usually from business pressure groups, to transfer taxes from themselves to other areas.

2. Governments are under pressure to increase expenditure on new areas of activity, or maintain expenditure in difficult times on areas that it was previously agreed to continue to spend money on.

Both these pressures can be simultaneous.

It is a rare, even non-existent motive that governments conclude that certain taxes are "inefficient" and desire to find alternative forms of tax, or despite protestations, wish to improve the design and efficiency of taxes. Old and inefficient taxes, unless the plucked geese hiss really hard, tend to last forever.

I hope that this book gets away from elaborating and permutating all the old taxes, same old, same old, as it recommends a single simple tax. Since the economic rent tax is the ultimate tax base, (called in economic circles the "ideal tax") there would be no loss in revenue if an economic rent tax was implemented to replace all other taxes. Furthermore there will be significant and very important efficiency gains. Also we can get away from this foolish and nonsensical idea that we have to "spread the taxes around". Ultimately incidence (a concept to be discussed later) makes all taxes a single tax anyway, but the process of incidence introduces a great deal of inefficiency. Finally the economic rent tax base is large, un-tapped, and can be a major source of permanent taxation revenue.

The advantages of a tax on economic rent

A major advantage of an Economic Rent Tax is the major increase in revenue, caused not by increasing the tax rate or taxing what was not taxed before, but regaining the losses to the economy caused by the so-called "Excess Burden" (to be discussed later) invisibly lost to the economy. This amount has been valued by researchers at least 20% of the total tax revenue raised.

Why should excess burden matter to you? The answer is simple. Increasing excess burden increases unemployment. At some point, actually quite low, you and many hundreds of thousands of others will lose their jobs as the value of the excess burden rises. Increasing unemployment is the direct consequence of raising the level of taxes. But the hidden tax, the excess burden, is by far the most harmful component of most taxes, and in most cases, the major cause of unemployment.

The book is divided roughly into two parts. Each part is of equal importance. The first part (Part A) discusses the practical aspects of taxing economic rents. The second part (Part B) discusses the more theoretical aspects of taxing economic rents. As a development of this discussion the book moves over to the subject of tax theory, and describes why a tax on economic rents is superior to most current taxes. The book finishes with describing the practical benefits of a tax on economic rents – the revenue gains, faster growth and a much simpler tax system.

PART A
PRACTICAL ISSUES

Chapter 1

Definition of Economic Rents

The theory of Economic Rents has an ancient pedigree by economic standards, going back to David Ricardo (David Ricardo 1817) who wrote on this subject at the beginning of the nineteenth century. Ricardo was investigating the role of land rents and the influence they had on wheat prices, and showed that increasing land rents did not increase corn (wheat) prices. If a landowner increased his rents, the farmer could not increase the price of corn by "passing on" the rent increase. In the long term, as many 'squeezed' farmers got out, the only option for the landowner was to reduce his rents to allow the farmer to have a 'normal' profit.

If on the other hand when wheat prices increased, landowners could grab the entire increase in profit, leaving the farmer with just his normal profit.

So the term "rent", while confusing to non-economists, has to be borne with. Economists are not any more willing to change the term than to stop using the QWERTY keyboard!

Definition. **Economic Rents** are the "return over and above opportunity costs or the normal return necessary to keep a resource in its current use". (Morton, John S, Rae Jean B. Goodman (2003), cited by Wikipedia). For our purposes this is one of the most useful definitions, one of scores of definitions available, as it ascribes "normal return", and opportunity cost as part of the definition.

Normal returns or normal profits are the minimum level of profits caused by competition that allow a business to stay in business. In a competitive friction free economy, with no market failures, all business will operate under the same rate of profit, the normal profit. If any part of the economy has a higher rate of profit, competition will cause resources to shift to that part of the economy.

Opportunity cost is the value of the best alternative activity foregone in a situation in which choice needs to be made between several mutually exclusive alternatives, given limited resources.

As you will immediately deduce, in the real world, above normal returns can and do occur, and continue to persist. In a real world economy, frictions and market failures are endemic, and cause firms to have a persistently high rate of profit. Or indeed a persistently low rate of profit that would cause firms eventually to exit from that industry.

A discursion on the subject of market failure

As this book will describe, economic rents are caused by something called "market failure". The definition of market failure is "an inefficient allocation of resources in a free market" (Wikipedia). In other words it is inefficiencies in the market system.

How do market failures cause economic rents? Economic rents are caused by the restriction of supply below the "equilibrium" level, as will be described a bit later in this book. As a consequence the price is raised above the equilibrium level. The product of the price difference between the equilibrium price, or the non-market failure price, and the market failure price, times the quantity sold at the market failure price is called in economics the "economic rent".

Now it is important to realize that market failures are a permanent feature of every free market system, and are even worse in a non-free market system. The market fails to adjust to eliminate "excess" prices. Permanent? Yes. Market failures are always with us. It is one role of government to try and reduce or eliminate market failure, through such activities as anti-monopoly regulation for example, but they can never be eliminated.

Up to a few years ago, economists treated economies with no market failures as not only "ideal", but "normal". They argued that free market economies trended to a situation where economic rents were zero, and called these temporary economic rents "Quasi Rents". Indeed a belief in the existence of quasi rents was tied up in ideological (Marxist) beliefs that the capitalist world was self destructing and profits were falling to zero. Modern economics has done away with this belief in the non-permanence of economic rents, and regard market failure as a permanent feature of any market economy. Indeed government intervention and macroeconomic policies would not work without market failures, and the major function of economists is to study them and how they affect economic activity.

Market failures and economic rents can be caused by:

1. Monopolies, cartels and non-competitive markets. These are the obvious cause, but there are many others that cannot be removed by government activity, or even by increased competition (*pace* the Marxists), including:
2. Time inconsistent preferences
   a. Decisions being made at different points in time can be inconsistent with each other depending on expected utility anomalies.
3. Information asymmetries
   a. One party has more or better information than the other. This creates an imbalance of power in transactions.
4. Principal agent problems
   a. An agent is motivated to act in his own best interests rather than those of the principal.
5. Externalities

      a. Cost or benefit that affects a party who did not choose to incur that cost or benefit, for example, manufacturing activities that cause air pollution impose health and clean-up costs on the whole society.
6. Public goods
      a. A good that is both non-excludable and non-rivalrous in that individuals cannot be effectively excluded from use and where use by one individual does not reduce availability to others.
7. Government policies, deliberately implemented, or accidently badly conceived and implemented
      a. Such as tariffs, taxes, subsidies, wage and price controls, regulations, and multifarious examples of what are called "government failure".

As can be seen there are a vast number of market failures in any market economy, no matter how free and unrestricted it is. All these market failures working together and individually create economic rents. As the rest of this book describes, these economic rents can be taxed. The erroneous belief that economic rents are due solely, or even mainly, to monopolies, cartels or non-competitive markets is complete nonsense. Shortages of goods and services are caused by numerous market failures raising the market price above the price that would occur, even if these monopolies, cartels and non-competitive markets did not exist.

Chapter 2

A Diagrammatic Explanation of Economic Rents

What does an economic rent diagram look like?

Economic rents can be described in terms of line diagrams. These basic diagrams for those not familiar with them consist of two axes, the vertical price axis P and the horizontal quantity axis Q. The diagrams consist of a "demand line" D going down from the top left, and a "supply line" S going up from the bottom let. Where these lines cross is the equilibrium price P. The shape and direction of these lines, and their shifts can be used to discern very interesting and useful conclusions.

The most basic diagram for economic rents, is a diagram with a vertical Supply line. In this diagram the land supply is inelastic. You cannot increase the supply of land no matter how much you increase the "rent" for land. (Though it has been found that when you start taxing the buildings upon that land, the supply line shifts to a non-vertical position, as you start taxing the supply of capital expenditure on buildings.)

DIAGRAM 1

Economic Rent
due to
Inelastic Supply

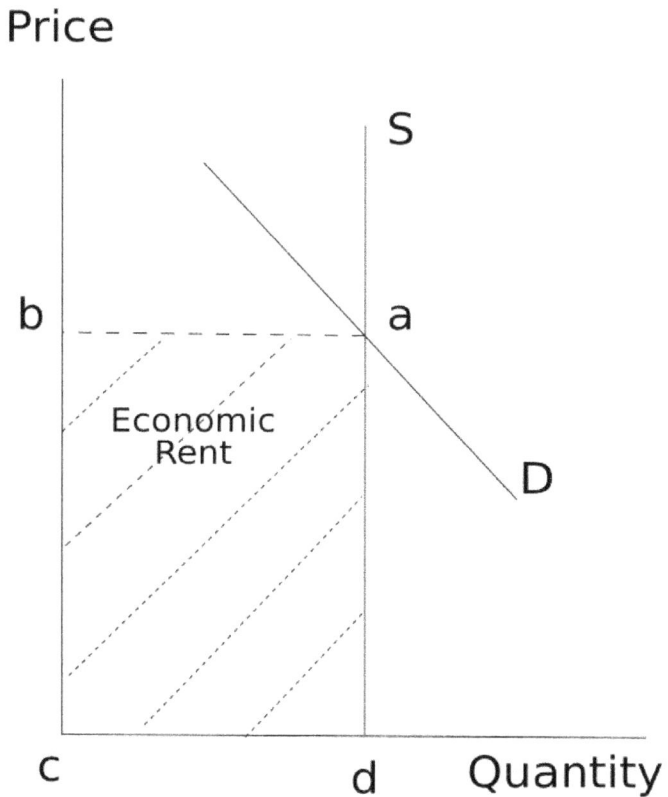

So you have a vertical supply line as in the diagram above. You cannot increase the supply of land.

So what does a more general economic rent diagram look like (with sloping demand and supply lines)?

DIAGRAM 2

Standard Theory of
Economic Rent

Price

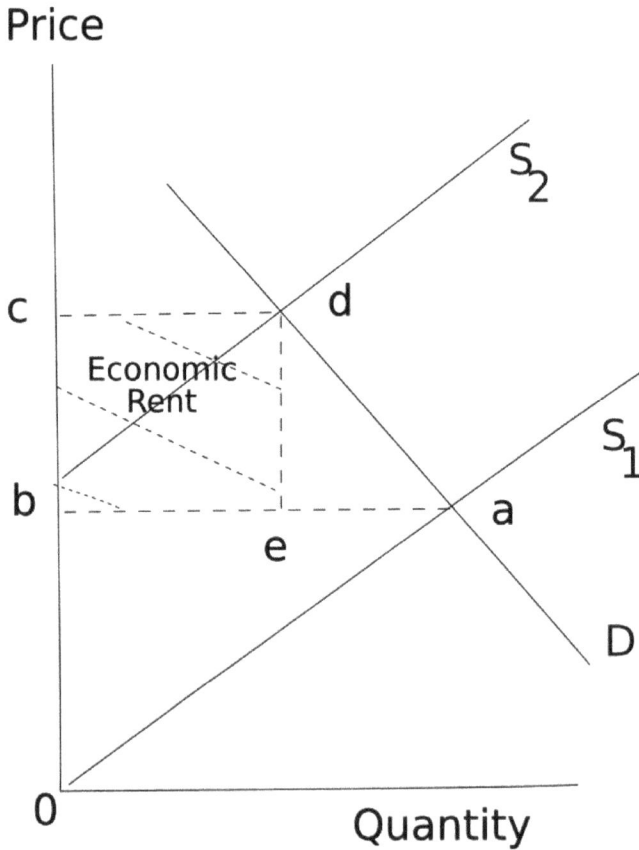

In Diagram 2 above, the equilibrium price is b. This is where there are no economic rents. Demand is completely met by supply. This is the equilibrium price, and one might call this the 'basic wage' in the employment market, though this can describe any market.

Now in Diagram 2, compared to the previous Diagram 1, you will note two supply curves S1 and S2. Supply has what economists call "shifted" from S1 to S2. Despite appearances the supply of goods has not increased. In fact at position *d*, less is supplied at a higher price.

The increase in price is the length *de*, and the size of the economic rent is *de* x *be*, or the size of the area *bedc*.

What can cause less to be supplied at a certain price, causing an economic rent? Yes, monopolies, cartels and artificial market restrictions will do that. But also that whole list of market failures above will also restrict supply and cause a rise in price and create economic rents.

And unlike monopolies or cartels and artificial market restraints, increase competition will have little or no effect on reducing the effect of these other market failures. They are a permanent feature of market economies, and create permanent economic rents.

Chapter 3

A Diagrammatic Explanation of Taxing Economic Rents

Using the Diagrams 1 and 2, the tax on economic rents can be very simply described. Take first the Diagram 1 with the vertical supply line, causing an economic rent due to a fixed land supply. Since you are directly taxing economic rent, you directly extract a chunk of the rent rectangle to tax, the rectangle *defc*. See below in Diagram 3.

DIAGRAM 3

Taxing Economic Rent
due to
Inelastic Supply

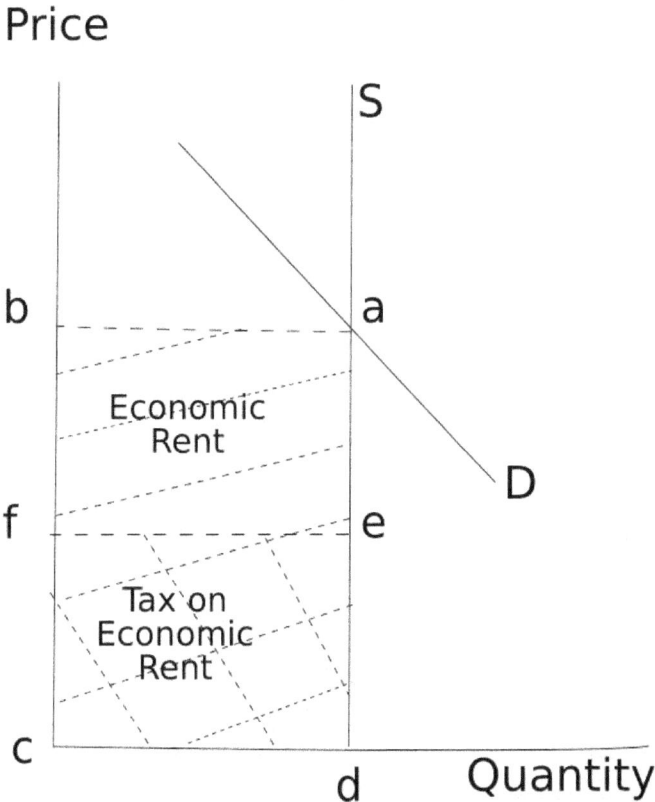

Price

b ————————— a

Economic
Rent

D

f —————————— e

Tax on
Economic
Rent

c

d Quantity

As can be seen there is a two-stage process. First the size of the economic rent is identified, area *cdab*. Then a tax is arbitrarily applied to that economic rent, area *cdef*.

Take the next diagram, Diagram 4, of the more general situation of economic rents, with sloping supply and demand lines. An economic rent area *cdab* is identified, and an economic rent tax, area *cdef* is applied.

DIAGRAM 4

Taxing Economic Rent
with sloping
Demand and Supply Lines

Price

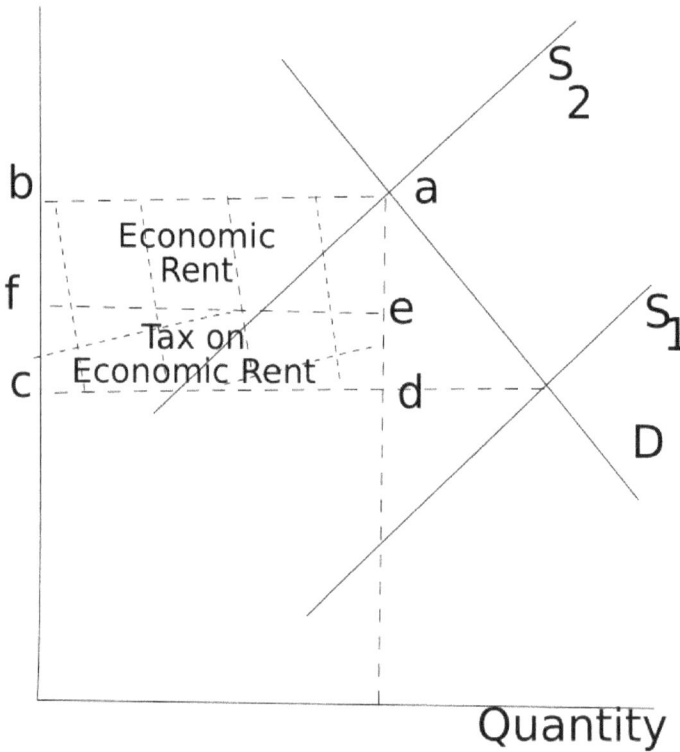

While an economic rent tax is conceptually very simple, the problem always has been to define and measure the size of the economic rent. This is covered in the next chapter.

Chapter 4

How to Calculate the Economic Rents for Businesses

While for over a century the concept of economic rents had important theoretical implications, measuring its actual value remained elusive. Then along came E. Cary Brown. Once in a while a totally obscure economics professor comes up with something earth-changing, a single written article, and then falls back to obscurity. Sometimes they keep up the good work, but in the case of E Cary Brown, while he continued to do good work, he made no further major discoveries in the study of economics.

What did E Cary Brown do? In an obscure article, part of a compendium of articles in an obscure book, written to celebrate the life of another economist, E Cary Brown (1948) described a methodology to calculate the economic rent earned by a firm. Economists, when they talk about profit, are only talking about "true" profit, which is to an economist can only be economic rent. Not the accounting profit, which everybody knows covers a multitude of sins. Every economist involved in providing investment advice knows accounting profits provide information varying between useless to downright deceiving. (Though how many times have you seen some idiot 'profit ratio' depending on some dodgy profit figure?)

What E. Cary Brown demonstrated was that the economic rent earned by a company can be calculated very simply. Note that this discussion is conducted in terms of calculating the Brown Tax base, which is equivalent to calculating the value of the economic rent of a company. A "Brown Tax" is the economist's jargon for a tax on economic rents. I shall use this term "Brown Tax" sparingly in this book, as it encourages ribald remarks from persons freshly introduced to the subject. It is unfortunate that the professor had the name Brown instead of Smith or Jones. Among its many consequences, it is virtually impossible to find a discussion of this tax on the internet due to interference from the many other Browns. So this book will refer to the "tax on economic rents", which is a clunky enough name. It is unfortunate that this tax is associated with difficult nomenclature.

Such an economic rent tax is classified by economists as "neutral". That means the imposition of the tax does not affect any economic decisions of the entity taxed such as investment or the choice between debt and equity.

The calculation formula

Variables required

The aim of this exercise is to define a set of variables for which you can obtain values from the Company Annual Financial Statement. Then plug these values into a simple formula. And lo! You have obtained the value of economic rents.

The Brown Tax Formula

The standard Brown Tax formula is - Economic Rents equals Revenue R, less, Expenses E less the interest payments i, and less the Capital Expenditure C. (For a mathematical proof turn to Chapter 18.) For those who want an even more rigorous mathematical explanation, I suggest that you turn to Boadway and Wildasin (1984), pages 321 to 331. There remains few better descriptions of this and related subjects.

The formula is:

$$\sigma = R - (E - i) - C$$ Where

σ is economic rent
R is total revenue
E is total current expenses
i is interest payments
C is total capital expenditure

Note the interest paid i is deducted from the Expenses E. In other words, unlike the current corporation tax, **interest expenses are not deductible!**

The other big difference is that capital expenditure **is 100% deductible**. In other words there is 100% depreciation on all capital.

Thus if a Brown Tax was introduced to replace the current corporation tax, there would be big differences. But remember we are not talking about taxes, but economic rents. To repeat, the Brown Tax base is the same as the value of the company economic rent.

So that's how you calculate economic rent.

Pedantic economists at this point will say that you can also calculate economic rents by deducting interest payments and economic depreciation instead from income less current expenditure. When you ask these pedants "How do you calculate economic depreciation?" you get only silence. Economic depreciation is impossible to calculate, and aggregate economic depreciation even more so. Accounting measures of depreciation come nowhere this figure, and impose a massive distortion on the tax system, generally discouraging investment. The only reliable method to estimate economic rents is the Brown Tax method.

There are minor issues with the definitions of the variables. These issues are explained below.

Step 1. The definition of revenue.

1. Total sales and service income. I prefer total or gross sales to net sales, as all returns etc. should appear under sales. Net sales is gross sales less the deduction of returns, allowances for damaged or missing good or any discounts allowed. The difference in practice is minor.
2. Add any sales of fixed capital assets.
3. Any cash revenue from any source.
4. This revenue figure must include all interest receipts.

Step 2. Deduct all the normal current deductions as conducted under the current Corporation Tax.
Except interest payments. Interest payments are NOT deducted!

Step 3. Deduct 100% of all capital expenditure for that year. That is, 100% depreciation or capital expensing. Wow! Isn't that good news?

The above is the standard Brown Tax base, and the measure of the value of economic rents.

A major issue is the treatment of **share issues** by the firm, **borrowings** and **repayment of borrowings**. The answer is simple. All capital increases by the firm are not considered part of the firm's income, and under a Brown Tax are not taxed. Therefore if a firm borrows, the cash inflow is not considered a part of its economic rent. Similarly a repayment of borrowings is ignored. Similarly the cash received by the firm from a share issue is not considered part of the firm's economic rents, and any share repurchases are ignored for the purpose of calculating economic rents.

In a later chapter (Chapters 18) I will go over the economic theory and mathematical proof the Brown Tax/economic rent base. If you get glazed eyes from the use of mathematics and economic theory jump over this chapter. You can also get economic advice from your friendly local economist. Warning – you will find it hard getting an expert in the subject of tax theory as this an arcane subject that few follow.

Chapter 5

Dealing with carry-forward losses

A common criticism of the Brown Tax is the issue of carry forward losses. There is a fear that as major capital deductions can be made at the start of a company's activities or at the start of a project, a major loss can occur that cannot be deducted against profits. What happens to these losses?

It is an implicit assumption that the Brown Tax applies symmetrically to years in which losses are made. For neutrality, it is said, the firm must receive a subsidy in these years, or a full loss off-set against its income elsewhere. This concept of a subsidy raises concerns that the government would then be a "partner" in the firm.

Neither requirement is necessary, for the simple reason that if the accumulated losses are carried forward until they can be set against subsequent profits, and furthermore interest is compounded on this carried-forward amount, this interest rate being that company's cost of finance, then the effect is neutral (Boadway and Bruce (1979)).

Thus the Brown Tax scheme is neutral as regards the investment decision of the firm. All the firm needs to do is deduct capital expenditure 100 percent, and carry forward any accumulated loses to deduct against future profits, making sure that interest at its cost of finance is compounded against this amount.

Such a procedure for carrying forward losses is allowed under the current corporation tax rules, even though the compounding of interest on accumulated losses is not allowed.

Chapter 6

How to Calculate Economic Rents for Employment Income

A Tax on Economic Rents of Employment Income

You can also have a tax on economic rents for **personal non-business income, including income from employment,** by taxing the personal income economic rent tax base.

This is treated separately from taxing business incomes as 1. normally in the case of personal employment you do not need to borrow to secure the job, and thus not pay interest. 2. Capital expenditure is not required, or if some expenditure is required, on tools etc. this is likely to be minimal.

Certain employment may in fact turn out to be more of a business – say types of contracting. In such cases, as will later be discussed, the solution is simple. The "business" is separated from the person, and is taxed separately. The person is paid a deductible salary from the business, and that income is taxed separately as employment income.

The personal income economic rent tax base is defined as the economic rents obtained by employment income above a threshold of income where no economic rents are accrued in that particular activity.

This threshold income can be defined arbitrarily as a "basic wage" of the lowest paid worker, or it can be found empirically – a wage level at which no discernable economic rents are accrued.

Thus this threshold wage level will be tax-free. Anything above this threshold income will be taxed.

The personal income economic rent base is defined as total income less the threshold income.

The tax rate can be progressive. Indeed it will be progressive even with a flat tax rate because of the tax-free threshold.

Chapter 7

How to tax the economic rent of land values

A Tax on the Economic Rent Component of Land Values

The third tax that is axiomatically a tax on economic rents is a tax on land values - the **"unimproved land value tax".** Note that I have not just said a "land tax". Much land, for example in the middle of the Nullarbor, carries no economic rents, and taxing that land at the same rate as in the middle of a city is economic nonsense. It must be stressed however, economic rent is a FLOW variable, and what you are actually taxing with the unimproved land value tax is the economic rent income component derived from the ownership of land.

However, in order to tax the unimproved land value base, take the total value of the property and deduct the value of "improvements", that is the value of buildings on that land, or in the case of rural properties, fences, pasture improvements, and so on. Once this is done, you get the unimproved land value.

The next step is to estimate the rate of return from that unimproved land value. This is the "economic rent". You then tax a component, or indeed what Henry George (Henry George 1879) wanted, all of this economic rent. Such a tax, assessed at a rate up to the value of the risk free rate of return on unimproved land values, is a tax on economic rents[1].

[1] Henry George, in his book "Progress and Poverty", published 1879, advocated that the values of unimproved land should be taxed to zero. He quite correctly pointed out that the land economic rents would then be re-distributed to incomes, and poverty would be vastly reduced.

Chapter 8

Separate the Economic Rent Taxes on Business Income and Personal Income

Under a Tax on Economic Rents, units operating a business have to be identified, and separated from the owner's personal income, and then businesses have to be taxed separately from personal income using the business economic rent tax.

The reason is not because an economic rent tax is a tax solely on business income. An economic rent tax can be applied on employment income also.

The reason is that there a basically two different ways of estimating economic rent:

These two different ways to estimate economic rents are
1. The method to calculate economic rents that have been created from business activities
2. The method to calculate economic rents accrued as part of employment income.

Both these methods have been described above. 1. The "Brown Tax" for business income, and 2. The excess over the basic wage for employment income.

Purists may argue that employees are trading in the economy and as such accruing economic rents. However, as employees do not generally invest in capital goods or borrow for employment activity, the Brown Tax method cannot be used to estimate their economic rents. So an arbitrary distinction has to be made.

Thus those activities earning rents through investment and borrowing activity have to be separated from those activities that do not.

In practical terms this distinction can be very simple. All those firms that wish to deduct capital expenditure and trade for a profit can be assigned a number, and those firms assigned this number will be taxed using the Brown Tax method. All other individual income earners are taxed the "excess income" method.

Though sometimes one and the same person would have both a "Brown Tax number" and also be taxed on "excess income".

I will give an example. Many doctors operate their practices on their own. Their practices are a business. Yet they draw personal income from their practice. With the current income tax the practice income and their personal income can be treated as one.

With an Economic Rent Tax, the practice business income and expenses have to be clearly separated from the personal income. The practice business can deduct capital expenditure at 100%, but must not deduct interest. The doctor can draw income from the practice business, and deduct this withdrawal of income from the business as an expense. He will then be taxed separately on his business to his private income with a separate economic rent tax on each type of activity.

Are drawings tax deductible for the business?

The example of the doctor's business leads us on to a very important practical question – how are business "drawings" taxed in the business? Or will they be treated as dividends, paid after tax is paid in the business?

Will the doctor be taxed again on the income he draws from the business? Under current law of the taxation of dividends, this dividend from taxed income could be "franked" and could be substantially tax free. Given the Doctors personal tax rate, the doctor would have to decide how much he would draw from the business to minimize his tax payments.

On the other hand, if the income drawn from the business is deducted **before tax**, this before tax income is added to the doctor's other before tax income, and the total income taxed as income appropriately.

Current taxation law, from my understanding, distinguishes the drawing between a salary paid by the business (paid before tax), or a dividend, (paid after tax, appropriately franked). Most small businesses, to my knowledge, under the advice of their accountants, utilise the first method. They draw the income as pay, and it is drawn from the business before tax.

For the reasons of simplicity I recommend the continuation of the second method when the business is treated as a separate entity under the economic rent tax system.

Are tax deductions allowed for personal income, especially interest payments?

Strictly speaking, no.

The simple reason is that a person who is gaining employment income is not operating a business.

In the case of interest, it can be argued that since the tax payer's economic rent is not estimated on a Brown Tax basis interest payments should be allowed. However there is a case that **no** deductions should be allowed for persons gaining employment income.

Under the current tax system deductions are allowed for two main reasons.

1. The activity of working as an employee is treated as a quasi-business, and activities such as education, even health payments, are treated as a form of investment aimed at improving income.
2. Some deductions are allowed as a means of improving the taxpayers' welfare, such as deductions for families and children.

Under an economic rent tax, the second category of deductions should not be necessary. If a person is earning economic rents that person should be capable of supporting themselves and their family without requiring further subsidies. If a person is earning below the economic rent tax threshold, they can be supported by further indirect welfare assistance.

Under the economic rent tax there is a strict distinction between business and non-business activities. A person earning employment income is not considered to be operating a business. If that person is also operating a business they should set up a separate entity to do so. No deductions should be allowed. Especially for interest payments. Otherwise there will be a tendency for interest deductions for investment activities to move from the business taxation area to the personal tax area. This would cause considerable distortions in tax administration.

Partnerships and trusts

Current taxation law taxes partnerships by dividing the taxable income among the partners, adding this taxable income to other taxable income of these individual partners, and taxing the partners separately.

Under the economic rent method, the partnership would be taxed as a business and would be assigned a number. The partnership would be taxed as a single entity, not as a group of partners, and the partners can then decide how much income they would draw form the partnership. As with the doctor above, this drawing could be franked and added to the individual partners income. They could then decide the amount they should draw to minimize personal taxation.

Alternatively, as described above, the partners' drawings could be paid as a salary and drawn before tax. Again, this is a far simpler method and this is the method I recommend.

Current taxation law treats trusts the same way as partnerships. The distributed income is divided up among the trust recipients and they are taxed separately from the trust. The trust is slightly different from a partnership in that it can accumulate income on behalf of the trust recipients tax free. Again as with a partnership, the trust would be assigned a number, and taxed on its earned economic rent.

For distributions for trusts to trust recipients, if the distribution with the current method is to treat distributions from the trust as before tax income, and it is added to the recipients' before tax income to be taxed appropriately by income tax, there is effectively no difference with the proposed method of distributing before tax income from the business.

The difference, and it is a major difference, is that under the present tax system trust income is tax-free. Under the economic rent tax system, trusts would be taxed as a profit making business entity.

The above is a very basic description of the tax on economic rents. The description will be elaborated and questions answered in detail later in this book.

Chapter 9

Calculating the potential size of an economic rent tax in Australia

Australia is used as an example in this book. However all countries would gain from moving over to solely a tax on economic rents.

I have no doubt a major economic catastrophe will be required to overcome the interests preventing change to an economic rent tax. But such a debacle will be sure to happen in the course of time due to the combined effects of excess taxation and excess borrowing.

There are two main reasons for introducing a universal economic rent tax in Australia:
1. Increasing growth
2. Increasing taxation revenue.

As has already been discussed, the present system of taxation incurs massive inefficiencies, and as such reduces economic growth and increases unemployment. Introducing an economic rent tax, and removing all or nearly all the other taxes will increase growth and greatly reduce unemployment. Increasing growth will also increase government revenue by the mere fact that economic activity has increased.

But will the introduction of an economic rent tax in itself, with no further provision for growth, increase tax revenue? In other words, would the elimination of inefficiencies inherent in the system such as excess burden release further income that can be taxed, assuming the rate of tax remains the same.

The way to answer this question this is to estimate the amount of tax that would be raised by a hypothetical tax on economic rents on both business and employment income, and compare it with the tax revenue actually raised in the same year.

In order to do this, it is necessary to choose a methodology to estimate economic rent tax revenue.

The reader may recollect that the formula used to calculate the value of the economic rent tax base is:

Value of the economic rent = Total revenue – Total Current Expenditure as normally described (including interest payments) – Total Capital Expenditure + Value of Interest Payments

Note: Current Expenditure does not include depreciation deductions.

It has been proposed in this book that capital expenditure can be estimated by deducting total assets in year one from total assets in year two, and adding back in the figure for depreciation in year two.

In actual practice there are problems with this. This lies with accounting practice or revaluing assets from year to year. Thus it is often the case that the estimated capital expenditure using this method is wrong, often wildly wrong. Indeed in those years when the value of the revalued asset in year two is below that of the value of the asset in year one, as in the year 2012-13, the economic rent base is massively expanded, as the negative capital expenditure is turned into a plus! A hardly realistic outcome for the tax base to greatly expand in years when the asset base is deceasing.

It is thus necessary to obtain an actual value of capital expenditure in each year.

Unfortunately the Australian Taxation Office (ATO), while it publishes the figure for Total Capital Expenditure for the Australian Economy in ABS 5625, does not publish this figure for the individual components of corporations, partnerships, trusts and individual businesses. Thus the economic rent base can be estimated for all Australian business, but not the individual components.

What is equally bad, the ATO, while it publishes total tax paid for Corporations, it does not publish the tax paid for partnerships and trusts, and for individuals the tax paid by businesses and employees is confused. The reason is that the ATO divides income from partnerships and trusts into income for the individual partners and trust recipients, and adds this amount into total income received by individuals. An economic rent tax system, would, as previously discussed, tax partnerships, trusts and businesses of individuals, as separate businesses and tax them just like corporations.

So the total economic rent tax of all business entities can be estimated as follows:

First let us state the total published capital expenditure in Australia.

ABS 5625 Private New Capital Expenditure
2012-13 Total new capital expenditure for all categories $160,520 million
taxstats@ato.gov.au

TABLE 1
Estimates of economic rent for each category prior to the deduction of capital expenditure for each category

Source: Taxation Statistics 2012-13 Companies Selected items

Corporations

Total Income	$2,714,909 million
- Total Expenses	$2,485,784 million
Net Income	$ 229,125 million
+ Total Interest payments	$ 163,989 million
Sum before deduction of capital expenditure	$ 393,114 million

Source: Taxation Statistics 2012-13 Trusts Selected items

Trusts

Total Income	$330,232 million
- Total Expenses	$304,528 million
Net Income	$ 25,704 million
+ Total Interest payments	$201,090 million
Sum before deduction of capital expenditure	$226,794 million

Source: Taxation Statistics 2012-13 Trusts Selected items

Partnerships

Total Income	$149,117 million
- Total Expenses	$130,509 million
Net Income	$ 39,608 million
+ Total Interest payments	$149,010 million
Sum before deduction of capital expenditure	$188,618 million

Source: Taxation Statistics 2012-13 Business income selected items

Sole trader income

Total Business Income	$97,644 million
- Total Business Expenses	$70,289 million
Net Income	$27,355 million
+ Total Interest payments	$ 916 million
Sum before deduction of capital expenditure	$28,271 million
TOTAL Sum before deduction of capital expenditure	$836,797 million
LESS Capital Expenditure from ABS Statistics	$160,520 million
Total Economic Rent for 2012-13	$676,277 million

Assuming tax rate of 30%
Estimated economic rent tax on business $202,863 million

Due to the lack of published capital expenditure figures for each of the above published groups it is not possible to estimate the economic rent taxes for each of the above groups.

But assume these taxes are proportioned among these groups in proportion to their Total Business Incomes.

TABLE 2

	Total Business Income millions	Proportion of total business income per cent	Proportion of total rent tax of $202,863 million
Corporations	$2,714,909	82.5	$167,306
Trusts	$ 330,232	10.0	$ 20,351
Partnerships	$ 149,117	4.5	$ 9189
Sole Trader	$ 97,644	3.0	$ 6017
TOTAL	$3,291.902	100.0	$202,863

This means that in 2012-13
- Corporations would have paid an economic rent tax of $167,306 million
- Trusts would have paid an economic rent tax of $20,351 million
- Partnerships would have paid an economic rent tax of $9189 million
- Sole traders would have paid an economic rent tax of $6017 million.

The corporate rent tax

The increase in tax receipts if an economic rent tax was imposed in 2012-13 would have been:

TABLE 3

Actual corporate tax	Estimated economic rent tax	Estimated increase in revenue	Percent increase
in 2012-13 million	in 2012-13 million	in 2012-13 million	
$64,530	$167,306	$102,776	159

Thus **Corporate** tax paid would massively increase, by about 159 percent or $102,776 million.

Would that increase hammer the company sector?

---

[2] There is a lot of empirical work on the subject. For instance there is tremendous amount of literature on contest experiments, It has been found that effort remains unabated even when the prize is scaled down. See Shmuel Nitzan 1994.

It has been found that oceanic fishers, who pay no tax, maintain the same effort even when fish stocks are depleting, until costs exceed revenue and economic rents are gone, and then they immediately stop fishing. See Karl K. Angelson, Steinar Olsen 1987.

Remember that now economic rents will be taxed. Economic theory says that such a tax will not slow the corporate sector one iota. A tax on economic rents does not reduce investment, nor, and this is more important, reduce the company's incentive to make a profit. The company has the same profit incentive regardless of the size of its economic rent. Even if the company has only one dollar of economic rent left it will be still be striving to make economic rents, and its conduct will remain unchanged as if it had one million dollars of economic rent. This may sound strange to non-economists. But economists do not relate the effort to achieve an above-normal return to the size of the above-normal return. On the other hand the size of a normal profit is related to the effort applied to achieve it. An economic rent is an economic rent, regardless of its size.[2]

Does maintaining the same "effort" mean that full employment is maintained until all the economic rent is gone? That is an interesting question that I will not attempt to answer here. But remember the current taxation system taxes both economic rents and normal profits, and this must have some effect on employment. Will taxation of economic rents maintain full employment (until all economic rents are gone)? Good question.

What about an expansion in activity?

The present corporate tax reduces the incentive to invest, and reduces the company's incentive to pursue profits as the tax rate rises. On the other hand, under an economic rent tax, the company's incentive to invest and expand would be unchanged as the tax rises.

True, if a company pays increased tax this would reduce its cash flow and ultimately its cash reserves. While it is not possible that even a tax on 100 percent of economic rents will drive a company into the ground (it will still be operating under "normal" profits), its capability to invest its supernormal profits in capital or expand its day to day activities will be in this case eliminated. Thus the situation is that a lower economic rent tax can lead to faster growth. There can be trade-off between the size of the economic rent tax and growth.

However, it could be argued that the present form of corporation tax leads to lower growth, and just to reach that same rate of growth under an economic rent tax, a higher rate of economic rent tax can be sustained.

Thus from the macroeconomic point of view an economic rent tax can be beneficial in two ways. 1. The economic rent tax may maintain full employment in a downturn as effort is fully maintained until all rents are eliminated. 2. Investment will be encouraged leading to faster growth.

Estimating income taxes paid by Trusts, Partnerships and Individual Business in 2013-14

It is an unfortunate result of the way the current income taxes are collected that this methodology has led to a very limited form of taxation statistics published by the Australian taxation Office (ATO). While nowadays corporation taxation statistics are published separately, personal income tax figures are published combined with taxes on Trusts, Partnerships and Individual Businesses. In other words, as Trusts, Partnerships and Individual Businesses are treated as the legal equivalent of the summed component of individuals, each individual in a Trust, Partnership or Individual Business is taxed separately as an individual. It should be remembered that an economic rent tax taxes each Trust, Partnership or Individual Business as a separate business. Thus under an economic rent tax, the ATO taxes would be completely different, being composed of taxes on Corporations, non-business or employment income of Individuals, Trusts, Partnerships and Individual Businesses.

Thus the ATO publishes the "Total tax levied on individuals", in ABS5506.0 – Taxation Revenue , 2013-14, which amounts to $159,021 million. This includes taxes on Trusts, Partnerships and Individual Businesses as well as employee income.

How does one separate these out?

Total income from all individuals, including Trusts, Partnerships and Individual Businesses in 2012-13, ABS5506.0, Taxation Statistics – Individuals: Selected Items , by Taxable Income and Total Income, 2012-13 Income Year is $705,592,441,747. (Note this sum is net of losses), or $705,592 million.

From above the total income from Trusts, Partnerships and Individual Businesses is

$330,332 million + $149,117 million + $97,644 million = $576,993 million.

Thus the total non-business individual income is $705,592 million - $576,993 million

= $128,499 million. (Yes, it is not often realized, but this is less than the income of trusts!).

The total income tax paid by individuals in 2012-13 was $159,021 million. This includes income tax paid by non-business individuals, Trusts, Partnerships and Individual Businesses.

Making the heroic assumption that all sectors pay taxes at the same rate, the taxes paid by each sector can be estimated.

Using the Table 2 and adding non-business individual income:-

TABLE 4

	Income $ million	% of total	Taxpaid $ million
Non-business	$128,499	18.2	$ 28,960
Trusts	$330,232	46.8	$ 74,425
Partnerships	$149,117	21.1	$ 33,607
Sole trader	$ 97,644	13.9	$ 22,006
TOTAL	$705,592	100.0	$159,021

Yes, that assumption that all sectors would pay equal rates of tax is probably heroic. It is probable that individuals would not involve themselves in Trusts unless there are major tax advantages, and businesses have opportunities to reduce their taxes. So the tax figures for the last three sectors would be probably on the high side. Nevertheless it is instructive to compare these figures with the potential economic rent taxes.

TABLE 5

	Rent tax $million	Current tax paid $ million	Gain/Loss (-) in tax paid $ million
Trusts	$20,351	$74,425	-$54,074
Partnerships	$ 9189	$33,607	- $24,418
Sole traders	$ 6017	$22,006	- $15,989
TOTAL	$33,557	$130,038	- $94,481

Thus the non-corporate business sector, that is the Trusts, Partnerships, and Individual Business would pay vastly less tax.

There is no doubt that the small business sector, that includes Partnerships and Individual Businesses pay too much tax under the present taxation system, and have paid much more than their economic rents. As for the Trusts, it is quite possible that they have been paying too much tax also, in excess of their economic rents. Many trusts operate farms, for instance, that possibly do not have high economic rents.

This analysis draws out the comparison between "big" business, that normally operates under high economic rents, and "small business" that does not.

Estimating economic rent tax on employment income

Using data from Taxation Statistics 2012-13. Individuals, Selected Items by taxable and total income

The ATO publishes its tax statistics in income groups. There are groups up to and including $30,000 per annum, and the next highest group is $30,000 to $37,000. There are a number of arbitrary choices, but it was decided to extract the Gross Tax and the Net Tax up to the income level of $30,000. For the total of these groups, total Gross Tax was $2556 million and total Net Tax was $1438 million.

My proposal is that economic rent for earned income is any amount earned over $30,000.

Thus there will be zero tax imposed on amounts earned under $30,000. For the sake of argument and simplicity any amount earned over that amount is taxed at the same marginal rate as the present tax, or that ruling in 2012-13.

Two points should be understood here about the issue of progressive taxes.
1. An economic rent tax can be taxed at a progressive rate. It is not necessary to tax an economic rent tax at a flat rate.
2. Even if an economic rent tax is taxed at a flat marginal rate, it is still a progressive tax. This is because if the tax free threshold is added to the total income the actual level of tax increases at a progressive rate as income rises.

Back to the statistics. Below $30,000 the total income taxed is $66,372 million and the total tax paid is $2,256 million.

Above $30,000 the total income taxed is $639,221 million and the total tax paid is $149,483 million.

Total tax paid currently is $151,739 million. The reduction due to a rent tax is $2,256 million. In percentage terms it is 1.5 per cent.

In actual terms the dollar value, if not the ratio reduction, is much less, as non-business individual income is only a fraction of total individual income, comprising of non-business individual income, Trust income, Partnership income and individual business income.

From the Table 4 non-business individual income is only 18.2 percent of the income of this group. Thus the reduction due to a rent tax is 18.2 per cent of $2,256 million, or $411 million.

Total economic rent tax income for non-business individuals would be 18.2 percent of $149,483 million or $27,206 million.

From this total economic tax revenue can be calculated, and compared to the tax revenue of the present system at the same rate.

Total Economic Rent Tax Revenue

Now comes the point where total economic rent tax revenue can be totaled up and compared to the total raised by the current taxation methods at the same rate.

I have not compared this with other sources of tax revenue such as the GST or excise as these cannot be directly substituted for a tax on economic rents. However a tax on unimproved land values is a tax on economic rents, and this can be substituted for a related tax such as stamp duties on profits, or can be used to replace an unrelated tax such as the GST.

The revenue raised by a tax on economic rents estimated in this book is shown in the following table, and compared to the actual revenue raised in the same year.

TABLE 6

	Estimated Tax on Economic Rents $ million
Corporation tax	$167,306
Non-business individuals tax	$ 27,206
Trusts	$ 20,351
Partnerships	$ 9,189
Individual business	$ 33,557
TOTAL	$257,609

The total economic rent tax revenue would be the total economic rent tax revenue from businesses (already calculated) plus total economic rent tax revenue from employment (calculated above). How much would this be?

The estimated economic rent tax on businesses is $202,863 million (Table 2).

How does this compare with the total tax raised from this group by the current taxation method?

The table for this is as follows. Note that current taxation statistics provide tax data on only two taxation groups, Corporation tax and tax on individuals. The group tax on individuals includes the sub-groups 1. Non-business individuals 2. Trusts 3. Partnerships 3. Individual businesses.

TABLE 7

Current taxation in 2012-13   (Source Australian Taxation Office Taxation Statistics 2012-13).

	Tax raised $ million
Corporation Tax	$ 64,530
Tax on Individuals	$151,739
TOTAL	$216,269

Thus imposing a rent tax is estimated to raise $257,609 million, an increase of 19 per cent over $216,269 at the present tax rates.

The major reason for the increase would be an increase in the corporation tax, which would more than compensate for a fall in tax on the various forms of individual income tax. Such a result is a clear indication that individuals are over-taxed by the present income tax system, and corporations under-taxed, using the criterion of taxing economic rents as a valid measure of the correct tax base to use.

PART B
OTHER THEORETICAL ISSUES

Chapter 10

The Reason Why Taxes on Economic Rents are Superior to All Other Taxes

To put it succinctly, there is no "excess burden" and there are no "incidence effects". The tax on economic rents is efficient. Thus in essence tax rates can be increased without the nature of the taxes themselves (as apart the quantity of revenue raised, and the nature of the expenditure – macroeconomic questions) having any adverse effects on economic activity. The economy would not be slowed by the inefficiency of the tax itself, as current taxation does, and thus these tax rises would not directly cause a rise in unemployment.

Current forms of taxation carry with it this hidden tax on a tax, this "excess burden". If there is a sudden shift to a tax on economic rents while retaining the current government "tax take", the return to the economy of the value of the current excess burden will increase growth and reduce unemployment.

The theory behind incidence and excess burden will be discussed later in this book. Suffice to say at this point, the concept is very simple. In fact all you need to measure both the incidence and excess burden effects are measurements for the elasticities of supply and demand for personal or business income being taxed. This is relatively a simple process, and economists have been using these elasticities to estimate incidence and excess burden values for the past forty years. By relatively simple, I mean compared to such processes such as general equilibrium estimates that are a lot more complicated to estimate.

Another important reason for instituting an economic rent tax on corporations in particular is that compared to the current corporation tax at the current rate of taxation there will be massive increase in tax revenue. An example of this is shown in the previous chapter.

If the reader finds this outcome unbelievable, the reason for this is simple. In all these years the value of interest deductions in the current corporation tax have greatly exceeded the value of capital expenditure. Remember, in the economic rent tax, interest is no longer deducted even though capital expenditure is. Thus the tax base is greatly increased.

An economic rent tax on employment income will also have beneficial effects.

All personal income can be divided into two components the non-rent component and the rent component. The lower component is the non-rent component, and the upper component is the rent component.

The rent component of personal income is defined by "income in excess of the minimum wage". The minimum wage is a vague and value laden definition. Karl Marx and others have defined this level as just above starvation level, or "subsistence", enough to keep an un-skilled worker fed and working, plus enough for his family, and allowing him to reproduce. Of course a lot of workers in the past have fallen below this level, and many governments since then have exercised themselves to define and impose a "minimum", or if the worker is unemployed, an necessary unemployment payment. It is not the purpose of this book to go into the methodology used to estimate these figures. Suffice to say estimates have been made, usually with the intent of providing an income above "subsistence" described by Karl Marx.

No matter whether economic rent is defined as wages above subsistence, or some higher figure defined by the government, it is still economic rent. As such economic rent has different characteristics from income obtained at below the minimum wage level.

Economists define the supply of work to gain income as "effort". Now economists do not think that there is a direct linear relationship between income and effort. They divide effort to gain income into two components. It has been generally found that all persons in order to gain more income put in more effort. However if income for some reason is reduced, if the income is above the economic rent threshold, effort is not reduced if income is reduced. However if income is below the economic rent threshold, effort is reduced when income is reduced.

Thus, if only income above the economic rent threshold only is taxed, effort will not be reduced regardless of the level of the tax. Indeed some economists have claimed that a tax rate of 99% will not reduce effort if it is applied to the economic rent component of employment income!

This result has been confirmed by many empirical and practical tests. Past an income threshold, people do not generally work "harder" due to increased pay. There are other discernable powerful motives to work harder – fear of losing the job, expectations of better things. This area is a vast subject in itself, and since it is not central to the subject of this book, I do not intend to spend time discussing it. There are many specialist labour economists who can advise.

However the main benefits of a tax on economic rents is the elimination of incidence effects and excess burden. These will be described in the next chapters.

Chapter 11

An Explanation of Incidence Effects

What is the definition of Tax Incidence?

"Tax incidence is an economic term for the division of a tax between the buyer and the seller." Investopaedia.

Analysis of Supply/Demand curves

The following is a technique that illustrates the application of tax theory using basic diagrams of Supply and Demand.

These diagrams, for those who are not familiar with them, consist of two axes. The vertical axis is conventionally the Price axis. The horizontal axis is conventionally the Quantity axis.

DIAGRAM 5

The Basic Supply/Demand Tax Diagram

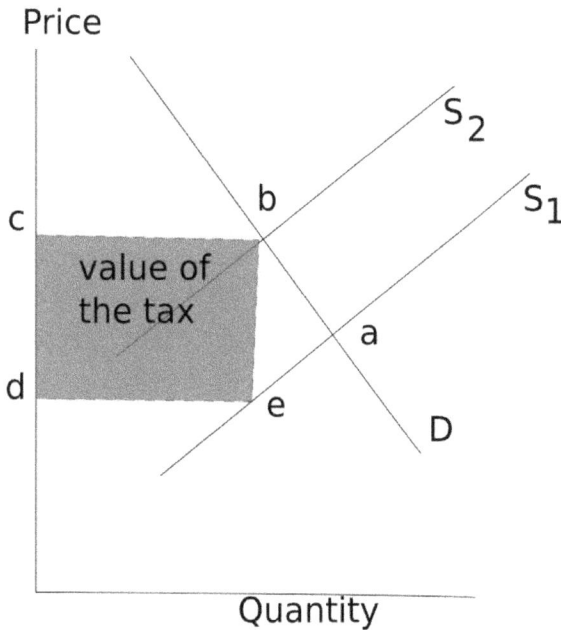

Price

S₂

S₁

c

b

value of
the tax

a

d

e

D

Quantity

The Demand line (denoted in the diagram by D) is most simply drawn as a straight line, going downwards from left to right. This means that as the quantity of the good increases, the price paid per unit decreases.

The Supply line (denoted in the diagram by S) is also most simply drawn as a straight line, going upward from left to right. This means that as to price increases, the quantity supplied increases.

These lines are made to cross, and the crossing point is called the equilibrium price.

When a tax is placed on a commodity, such as a sales tax, the price of the Supply increase per unit quantity. This causes the Supply line to move upward parallel from right to left. The Supply line moves from S1 to S2.

Now the tax per unit is the vertical distance between the Supply lines S1 and S2. It is the distance in this diagram *eb*. The total quantity of goods sold after the tax is applied is the distance in this diagram *ed*. Thus the total value of the tax is the shaded area, the tax per unit times the quantity of goods sold, or the area of the rectangle *ebcd*.

Simple. But that is not the end of the story.

DIAGRAM 6

The incidence of a Tax on a Commodity divided between the Buyer and the Seller

Price

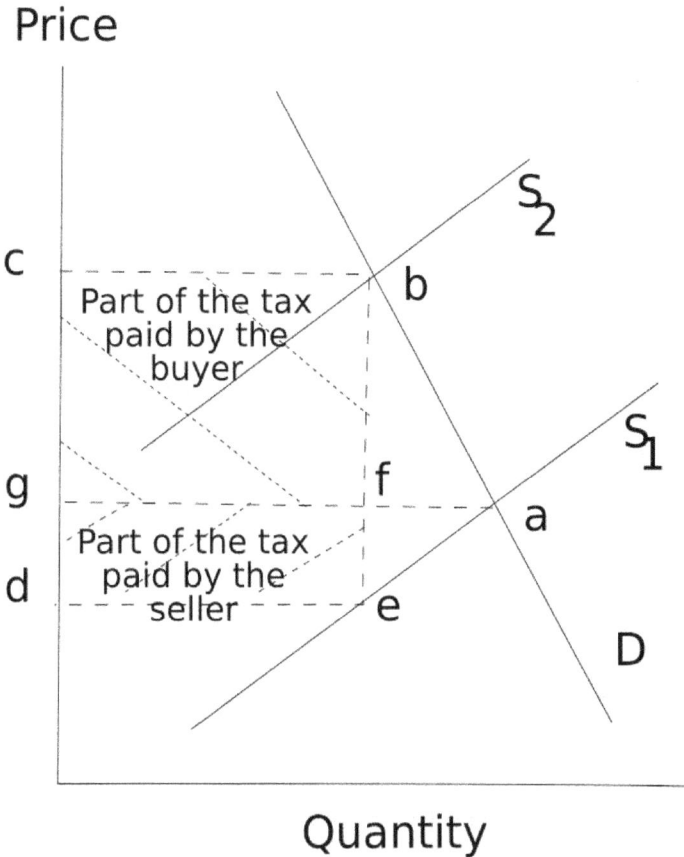

Quantity

If you draw a horizontal line from *a* to *g* through *f* you split the area of taxes in two, though not necessarily equally.

The bottom rectangle *efgd* is that part of the tax which is paid by the seller. The top rectangle *fbcg* is that part of the tax which is paid by the buyer.

This division of taxes is called the "incidence" of the tax.

The essential point to remember is that, unlike the usual assumption by all non-economists, the buyer does NOT pay all the sales tax. Part of this is passed onto the seller. The tax per unit *be* is divided into two parts: that which the seller pays, *fe*, and that which the buyer pays, *fb*.

Incidence is an important component of taxation. The lesson is that those who *nominally* pay the tax are not those who *actually* pay <u>all</u> the tax.

The following is a different sort of diagram, showing the taxation of income.

Here again the supplier is taxed (the employee), but we assume a progressive tax, where the rate of tax rises from zero to whatever. (These diagrams can be designed of all sorts of scenarios). The Demander is the employer.

DIAGRAM 7

The Incidence of an Income Tax

Price

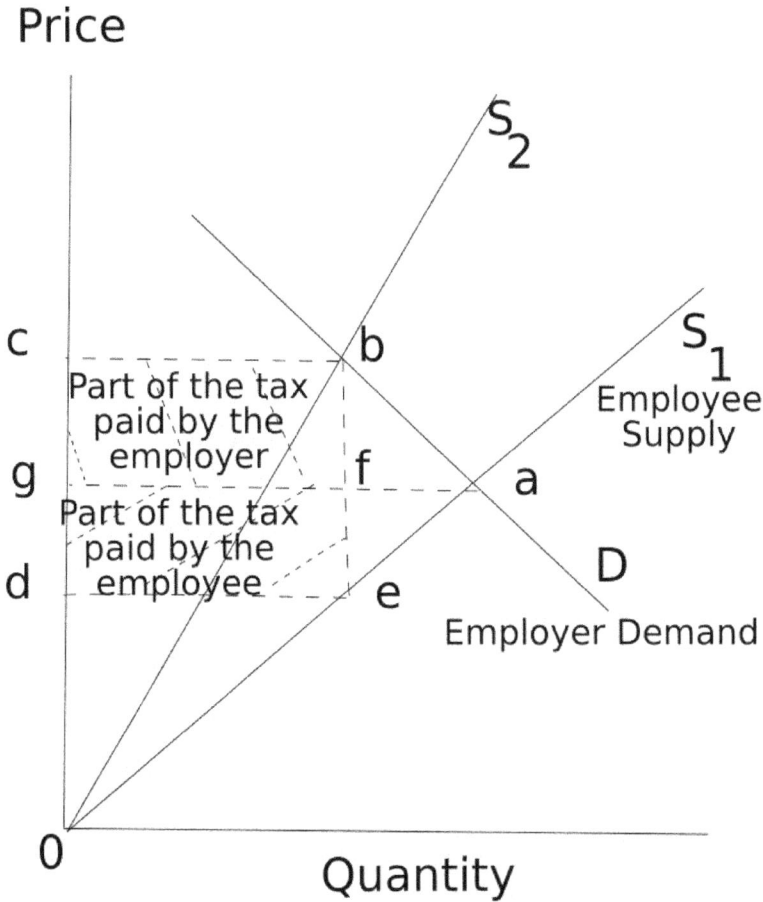

Again as can be seen, the tax is length *eb* at point *b*, total tax *ebcd*. But the income tax is divided between the employer and the employee. The employee pays *efgd* and the employer pays *fbcg*.

Corporate taxation? If a corporation tax is imposed on a company it increases its average costs, which increase the company's marginal costs, which in turn could shift the firm's Supply line upward. The nature of this shift depends on the firm's pricing policy. (It is a myth that the marginal cost curve is the firm's supply curve – that depends on pure competition and decreasing returns to scale).

Thus the effect of a corporate income tax is more or less the same as the diagram of the tax on a commodity. The corporation, the supplier, pays the proportion *efgd* of the total tax *ebcd* and the corporation's customers pay the proportion *fbcg*. In other words, the corporate income tax is split between the corporation and its customers.

DIAGRAM 8

Incidence of a Company Tax

Price

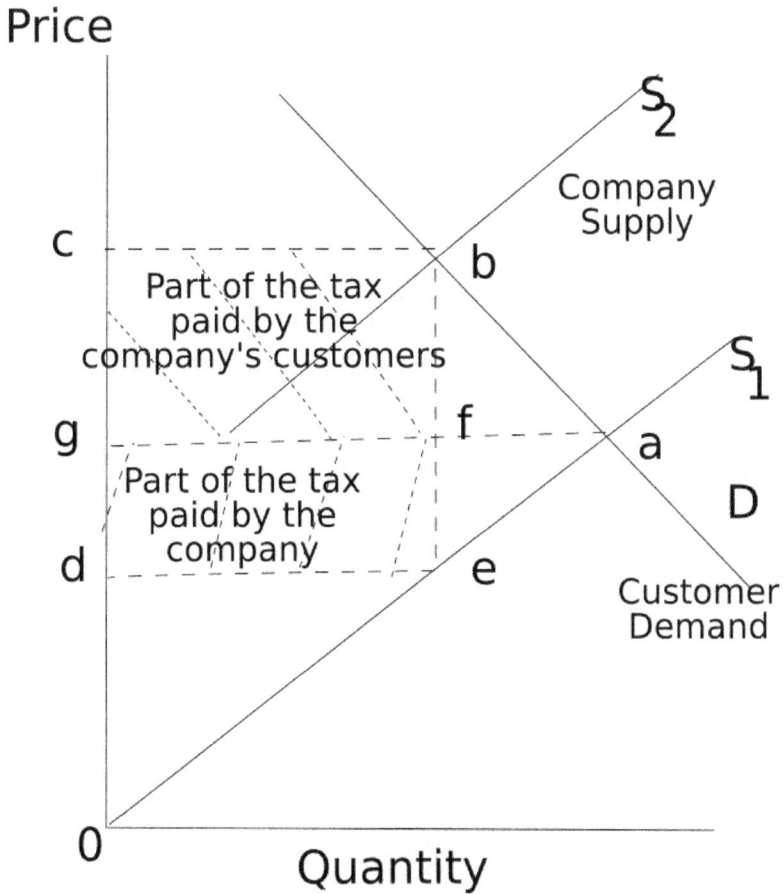

S_2

Company
Supply

c

b

Part of the tax
paid by the
company's customers

S_1

g

f

a

D

Part of the tax
paid by the
company

d

e

Customer
Demand

0

Quantity

Incidence and elasticities

So what is incidence? Incidence is the technical name for "tax shifting". If a tax is imposed on a certain taxpayer, many taxpayers are able to shift part of the tax onto somebody else. This is done by price changes in the economy and not consciously by the taxpayer. Thus if the taxpayer is fortunately situated, even if he/she nominally pays the tax, part or nearly all of that tax is recouped from other buyers and sellers by the effect of price changes. The size of this tax shift depends on the hidden market power of the taxpayer.

How much of this tax is shifted? The proportion of the tax that is shifted depends on the slope of the supply and demand curves. If a commodity or income tax is imposed, if you have a nearly vertical Supply or Demand line, a high proportion of the tax stays with or is shifted to the one with the most vertical line. (I could provide another diagram to show this, but I am trying to keep this book as short as possible. Get an expert to draw further explanatory diagrams as needed).

In economic parlance these slopes are called 'elasticities'. A near vertical slope means that supply or demand is inelastic. Essentially if Supply or Demand is inelastic, quantity changes are unresponsive to price changes.

The horrible example of Woolworths shifting the sales tax

Non-economists tend to smile at the term elasticity. But elasticities and inelasticities have serious consequences. I shall give an example. Take the example of Woolworths. Woolworths' customers have a very elastic (price responsive) demand, but Woolworths itself has a very inelastic (non price responsive supply – it will supply the same quantity at whatever price the customers are willing to pay). So what happens to a Goods and services Tax (GST) (a value added sales tax imposed in Australia) imposed on the goods it sells? The major part of the value of the GST is passed from the customers (with elastic Demand), on which it is exacted, onto Woolworths (with inelastic supply).

But that is not the end of the story. Woolworths has suppliers. As Woolworths' suppliers are many and competitive, Supply to Woolworths is very elastic. That is the Supply line is nearly flat.

It is likely that Woolworths' Demand line is a lot more inelastic, as it can be a lot more discriminatory about the prices it offers. Woolworth's Demand line is more steep.

Now as Woolworths has effectively incurred a loss of income due to the GST (it was not able to push the prices up to cover all of it), it passes this on to its suppliers by offering reduced prices. Woolworths Demand line falls to the left.

Now the incidence of the price fall can be worked out. It has interesting effects. While the lower 'rectangle' is still the suppliers, and the above 'rectangle' is still the buyer, the role of the elasticities reverses. The sellers, even though they have the more elastic Supply line, now absorbs a higher proportion of the price fall. The buyer, (Woolworths), even though it has a more inelastic Demand line, absorbs a smaller proportion of the price fall imposed by the GST. (Thus it does make a small loss).

So in this case Woolworths manages to pass on most of the GST to its suppliers. (Remember the sellers' (Woolworths' suppliers) rectangle is the bottom one and Woolworths' buyer's rectangle is the top one).

This is the hidden reason why Woolworths' suppliers' prices and profits are squeezed, and there are so many squeals and complaints. Despite the suppliers ostensibly passing the GST up the supply chain, it is then passed back down the supply chain to rest on the original supplier.

I shall leave the construction of both diagrams as an exercise for the reader. There is not enough space in this book for numerous diagrams.

If a GST of 10 per cent is charged on fresh food, the effect on farmers' profits will be horrendous. They WILL certainly see a near 10 per cent drop in prices in goods supplied to the major stores.

The introduction of the GST is the consequence of accepting bad and (mistakenly) self-interested advice based on outdated textbooks. The manufacturing members of pressure groups (that promoted this tax) in the end now pay most of this tax in actuality, not the consumers!

Is there any way to stop this form of inefficiency? Yes there is. As will be shown later in this submission, a tax on **economic rents** has **no** incidence effects. Why? When you are taxing economic rents you are not really taxing income, you are taxing a different animal, an economic rent. The supply and demand lines does not shift, and so you cannot get any incidence effects. The tax stays with the entity that actually pays the tax, and cannot be passed on.

Furthermore this *tax shifting* carries inherent cost. While the costs of the *process* of shifting taxes have not really been measured, though they are likely to be high, the costs of taxes in an inefficient configuration have been estimated, and these costs are substantial. These costs come under the heading of "Excess Burden".

Chapter 12

An Explanation of Excess Burden

What is the definition of Excess Burden?

"Loss of economic activity due to the imposition of a (structurally inefficient) tax compared to a free market with no tax." Farlex Financial Dictionary, 2012, Farlex Inc.

The theory of Excess Burden goes back to Hicks, but two current major authorities are Auerbach and Hines (2001) Feldstein (2008), who have each written many papers on this subject.

So what is Excess Burden, otherwise known in the literature as the Deadweight Loss? I turn again to the diagram previously described for the Incidence Effect. In this diagram however, to the right of the line *be*, made by dropping a line from the intersection of the second supply line and the demand line, is a triangle made by the demand line, the first supply line and the line be.

What is the meaning of this triangle? This triangle describes an area of invisible loss caused by imposing the tax. The value of the tax imposed is the area *bcde*. However the loss to the taxpayer caused by the shift of the supply line upwards is the area *bcdea*. This loss is over and above the amount of the tax value *bcde*. This loss was traditionally known in economic analysis as the 'deadweight loss', but in taxation analysis it has come to be called 'excess burden of taxation', a term initially coined by Harberger (1971), and this area is often called the 'Harberger triangle'.

DIAGRAM 9

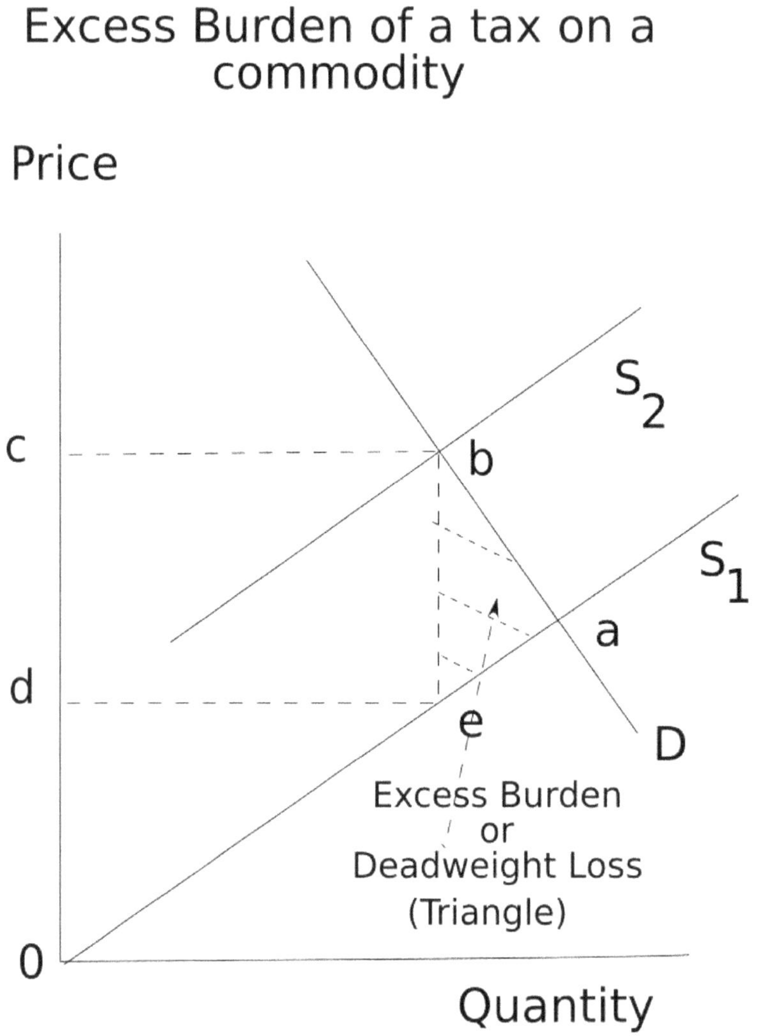
Excess Burden of a tax on a commodity
Price
S2
c
b
S1
a
d
e
D
Excess Burden
or
Deadweight Loss
(Triangle)
0
Quantity

So what is happening in the above diagram?

In this example a sales tax is imposed, such as a GST, at an amount *eb*. This has the effect of moving the Supply line up from S1 to S2, as the cost is increased. Aside from the incidence effects described in the previous section, the tax causes the loss triangle *abe*.

As can be seen from the above triangle, these losses are not negligible. In this diagram it is about 20 per cent of the total tax paid.

Now I often get asked "What does excess burden mean to me. I instinctively understand tax shifting, but how does excess burden affect the butter on my turnips?"

I reply "As the definition says, Excess Burden is a loss of economic activity. In other words economic activity is reduced, economic growth is reduced, and you may even lose your job as a consequence. Excess burden is not nice, it is real, and it can have major nasty effects that can impact directly upon you."

This Excess Burden is a hidden loss to the economy. It cannot be directly measured in terms of tax dollars, but there are methodologies available which can indirectly estimate this amount. But, even though the Excess Burden loss appears "theoretical" it has a very real loss on the economy, and this amount can be estimated. Its effect is just like the tax imposed by the enemy power discussed earlier, it is money and resources taken from the economy and it is not returned. Unlike most taxation, Excess Burden is a net loss to the economy. Thus the effect of a 20% Excess Burden is far more serious than a 20% normal tax imposed on the economy, as the latter tax is normally paid back into the economy.

DIAGRAM 10

Division of the Excess Burden between
the Buyer and the Seller

Price

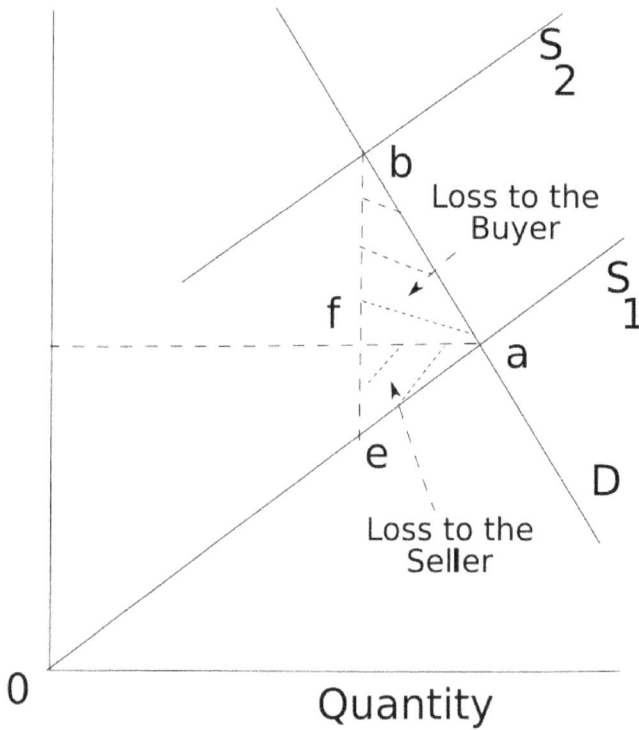

S_2

b

Loss to the
Buyer

S_1

f

a

e

D

Loss to the
Seller

0

Quantity

Excess Burden does not drift out into "the economy" as many textbooks imply. A vague loss to the economy. It lands on the transactors, people and businesses. Excess burden, as with incidence is divided between the buyer and the seller. In the above diagram, the excess burden loss to the seller is the area of the triangle *afe*, and the excess burden to the buyer is triangle *afb*. Both these triangle vary in size according to the slope (elasticity) of supply and demand. As Demand becomes more inelastic the proportionate loss to the buyer increases, but the total excess burden falls. Similarly, as the supply becomes more inelastic the proportion of the excess burden loss to the seller increases, but the total excess burden declines.

So, both the buyer and the seller are worse off. They lose. Directly. They have less money, much more than the value of the tax. Economic activity shifts along the demand line. The seller sells less, and the buyer buys less.

DIAGRAM 11

Excess burden due to income Tax

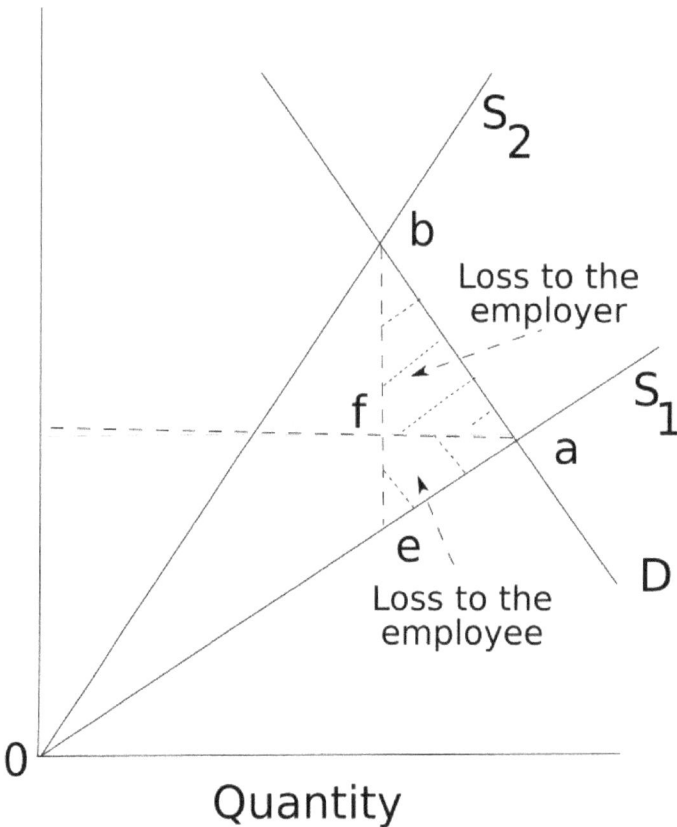

Excess Burden due to
Income Tax

Price

S₂

b

Loss to the
employer

f

S₁

a

D

e

Loss to the
employee

0

Quantity

Excess burden can also occur with income tax. In the above income tax diagram the value of the excess burden is the triangle *aeb*. The excess burden is divided between the employee and the employer. The excess burden loss to the employee is the triangle *afe*, and to the employer *abf*.

Again, if the Demand for the employee's services are inelastic, most of the excess burden is borne by the employee. On the other hand if the Supply of employment is inelastic, most of the excess burden is borne by the employee.

The economic activity of the employer is reduced, and the quantity of employment demanded of the employee is reduced. Both are worse off.

Minimising Excess Burden losses

Are there any situations where excess burden losses a minimized, indeed reduced to zero?

We are now going in the direction where this book is headed. Yes there are three situations where there are no excess burden effects:
1. Where the supply is perfectly inelastic
2. Where the demand is perfectly elastic and
3. Where economic rents are taxed.

Now, while perfectly elastic demand and perfectly inelastic supply is not found in real life, near inelastic supply is found. An example of a perfectly inelastic supply is that of land. However more recently it has been found that the supply of land is not quite inelastic (Prest 1981). The reason why the empirical measure of the supply of urban property was found to be not quite inelastic was that the supply of the buildings on the land was found to be more elastic. The supply of land and the supply of buildings on them have to be separated.

This will be discussed further in the concept of 'unimproved land values', as tax on unimproved land values is a tax on economic rents, and excess burden is eliminated.

Chapter 13

The Costs of Excess Burden

Measuring the Excess Burden

Now these losses are not as I said something theoretical and do not exist. These losses exist and can be **measured.** They depend of course on the elasticities of supply and demand. (This is why I gave a somewhat didactic course in economics in the above section. It is essential to understand the meaning of the elasticities of Supply and Demand, what is Incidence, and what is Excess Burden).

So what are these losses? Have they been measured?

At this point I will say that two types of deadweight losses can be measured, the average deadweight loss, which is the size of the above triangle, and the marginal deadweight loss, which is a measure of the incremental change of the average deadweight loss as the tax value changes.

While economists love the marginal deadweight loss, in order not to confuse the punters I shall stick to average deadweight loss. Suffice to say marginal deadweight losses have been measured as two to three times the average deadweight losses, so there is no respite from this analysis by going in that direction.

A useful summary of the measures of average deadweight losses is in the CIS Report "Cost of Taxation", (Robson 2005) Robson provides a couple of useful tables. These are:

Table 8: US Estimates of the Average Deadweight Costs of All Taxes

Study	Estimate Percentage of the tax
Ballard et al (1985)	23.8%
Jorgenson and Yun (1990)	21.2%
Jorgenson and Jun (1991)	18%

This is not an insignificant amount. We are just talking here about the "Economic cost", not the Administrative and Compliance costs. These fall directly on the taxpayer. While these have not been discussed in this book, for most taxes they can be significant in themselves, ranging around 15 to 20% of the tax raised. However Administrative and Compliance costs for taxes on economic rents are likely to be much lower as the economic rent taxes are much simpler. As they are simple in design they are likely to be much easier to administer than the numerous complex taxes they can replace. All these costs, both economic and administrative, can be substantial. And yes, they massively impact by slowing down the economy and increasing unemployment.

But back to deadweight losses. It is worth quoting Robson "Taxation for all levels of government in Australia in 2003-04 was $257 billion. Applying US estimates of the Average Deadweight Costs to Australia suggests that the total excess burden of taxation in Australia in 2003-04 amounted to at least $46 billion and could be as large as $61 billion. To put this in perspective, in 2003-04 government at all levels spent $51.5 billion on health. Thus the total deadweight loss from taxation in Australia, not including costs associated with administration, compliance and evasion is approximately equal to the amount of public spending devoted to health".

The latest Australian Tax Office figures, for 2013-14, give total taxation revenue for all levels of government as $434 billion. This gives a total excess burden ranging from $78 billion to $87 billion. Total Health spending in 2013-14 was $65 billion.

Or to put it another way, if excess burden is removed, the economy would expand by up to $87 billion. If tax rates remain the same, or total taxes increase pro rata, this will go a long way to cover the expenditure on Health.

The Average Deadweight Cost has also been calculated for income tax. These have been reported by Robson in the following table:

Table 9: US Estimates of the Average Deadweight Cost of Personal Income Taxes

Study	Estimate Percentage of tax revenue
Hausman (1981)	18.4% - 22.1%
Ballard et al (1985)	37.4%
Jorgenson and Yun (1990)	33.3%
Jorgenson and Yun (1991)	18%
Feldstein (1999)	32.2%

While these results are quite old, some useful recent theoretical studies are below.[3]

---

[3] J. Creedy 2003 "*The excess burden of taxation and why it (approximately) quadruples when the tax rate doubles*". New Zealand Treasury Working Paper, 03/29 December 2003. Unfortunately the paper includes no measurements.

Followed by J. Creedy 2004 "*The excess burden of taxation*". Australian Economic Review, Vol (37) (4), p454-464. This is an excellent description of the theory of excess burden. To quote a basic conclusion "Hence the excess burden is approximated by one half of the Hicksian Elasticity, multiplied by post-tax expenditure, multiplied by the square of the proportional tax-inclusive rate of tax. That means for example, doubling the rate of tax quadruples the excess burden."

Also J. Creedy, 2009 "*Personal income taxation: from theory to policy*" Australian Economic Review, Vol 42, (4), pp 496-506.

Charles Ballard, Don Fullerton. John Shoven and John Whalley, 1985, "*A General Equilibrium Model for Tax Policy Evaluation*", The University of Chicago Press,Chicago. They say "The deadweight loss increases with the square of the tax rate, and linearly with elasticities".

An interesting theoretical paper. Raj Chetty "*Is taxable income elasticity sufficient to calculate deadweight loss?*", American Economic Review – Public Policy 1(2):31-52, 2009.

The Effect of Excess Burden on the Economy

So far the discussion on Excess Burden has been somewhat theoretical. But this discussion can be clothed finally in a somewhat more practical and dramatic conclusion. Early on, in the section on Measuring the Excess Burden, it was shown that the Average Excess Burden in the United States was around 20% of tax revenue.

In the same section it was remarked that both John Creedy and Charles Ballard found that deadweight losses increase with the square of the tax rate. This tax rate can either be the marginal tax rate of a particular tax if you wish to estimate the deadweight loss of the tax at that point, or if you wish to estimate the deadweight loss for the entire economy, a rough and ready approximation is the average tax rate for the economy. The proportion of tax to GDP.

The proportion of tax to GDP in the US is 26.9% (source Wickipedia). In Australia this proportion is often given as 28.48%, of total taxation, Federal, State and local, in Australia.

Tax statistics[4] are	million
Commonwealth Government Revenue	$351,522
State Revenue	$ 68,720
Local Government Revenue	$ 14,738
Total Revenue	$443,885

Australia's GDP in 2013/14 was $1,558,334 million

Proportion of Total Revenue to GDP in Australia was 28.48%.

The relation of the Tax Rate to the Deadweight Loss or the Excess Burden can be described in a formula

$E = aT^2$

Where E is the percentage of the Excess Burden to GDP and T is the Tax Rate

---

[4] ABS 5506, Total Taxation Revenue 2013/14

This is the formula of a parabola with the vertex at position (0,0).

The Excess Burden for the US is about 20% and the Tax revenue to GDP ratio was reported as 26.9%.

Thus $20 = a (26.9)^2$

So a = 0.0276392

These values have been calculated in the following table using the above formula and substituting for a.

TABLE 10

T % Tax to GDP ratio	E % Excess burden **percentage of the tax**	T% x E% = C% Excess burden **proportion of GDP**	T% + C% Add tax ratio to GD to excess burden ratio to GDP
0	0.00	0.00	0.00
5	0.69	0.0345	5.03
10	2.76	0.414	15.41
15	6.22	2.212	29.32
20	11.06	4.3175	37.46
25	17.27	7.464	29.31
30	24.88	11.858	37.46
35	33.88	25.1865	46.86
40	44.22	17.688	57.69
45	55.97	25.1865	70.19
50	69.10	34.55	84.55
55	**83.61**	**45.9855**	**100.99**
60	99.50	59.7	119.7

DIAGRAM 12

Chart of tax rate % of GDP to Excess Burden % of tax

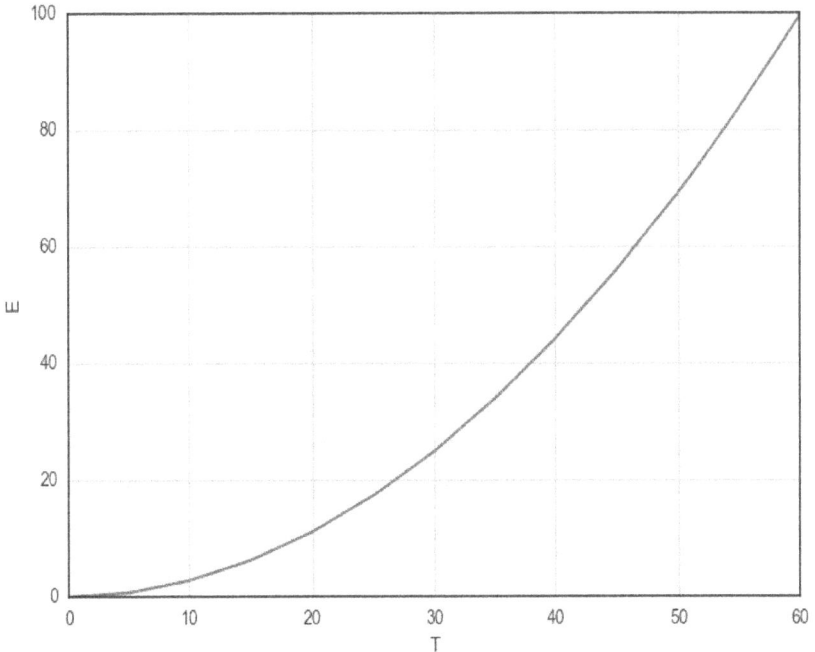

E is Excess Burden % of Tax

T is Rate of taxation % of GDP

Rate of taxation % of GDP is a proxy for the average tax rate.

While these results are rough and ready they demonstrate two essential points. First, shortly after you go past the present tax to GDP ratio in the US of 26.9% or in Australia of around 28%, the Excess Burden of is around 20% of the tax. The Excess Burden then accelerates rapidly.

The second point is that the "total catastrophe point" is comparatively low. When the proportion of tax to GDP reaches 55%, the proportion of Excess Burden to GDP equals 46%, and then the total of tax plus excess burden is 100%! The tax regime takes everything.

In time of war Britain never managed to increase its average rate of tax past about 55%, and had to rely on borrowing. Today, most high tax countries have a problem raising further tax revenue and have to raise further revenue by borrowing or printing money, until they inevitably run out of credit. All countries have a measurable limit on both taxing and spending, and must arrange their spending priorities within those limits.

Such a measurable limit in taxation is shown by the peak of the Laffer Curve, an inverted 'u' showing the relationship between rising and falling tax revenue and the increasing average rate of tax. I have derived a Laffer Curve formula, a cubic curve, from the concept of excess burden, and have found that the peak of the Laffer Curve in the USA is at an average tax ratio of 33 percent of GDP. After that, tax revenue falls as the average rate of tax increases. At the moment the USA has an average tax ratio of 27 percent of GDP, so this peak is not far to go. This could be one reason why this and many other governments are so dependent on borrowing – they can't raise more revenue by taxation no matter how hard they try.

This curve goes through the zero tax revenue axis at about at an average tax ratio of 66 per cent of GDP, assuming the curve is even-sided and there is no kurtosis.

Describing this development of the Laffer Curve in detail is too much of a diversion on the subject of this book. If I have not published a paper on the Laffer Curve in a journal in the near future I shall publish a monograph on the subject.

This book now moves on to a number of chapters, which while containing related issues, are not essential to the core of this book. Nevertheless this coverage is necessary, as they refer to matters that are related to the economic rent tax.

Chapter 14

The fallacy of Quasi Rents

Quasi Rents – a false belief

The term "Quasi Rent" has been around a long time (especially in bad textbooks). The definition of Quasi Rent is "temporary economic rent". Why temporary?

For many years economists have agonized for ideological reasons (Marxist) that long tem economic rents do not exist in a market economy, and if any economic rents exist they are purely temporary and will fall back to zero quickly. For this temporary rent, they coined the term Quasi Rent.

In fact most economic rents are not caused by monopolies, cartels and lack of competition, but by other market failures discussed previously in this book. These market failures, such as information asymmetries or agency problems, are a permanent part of the market economy and do not decline over time. The economic rents they cause are significant, probably cumulatively larger than those caused by lack of competition. (Amit and Schoemaker (1993))

The belief in quasi rents is central to Far Left ideology. Karl Marx wrote that over the course of time all profits would be ground down to zero by competition, and a revolution would result when workers would seize control of all factors of production. Thus a belief in low and falling economic rents is at the back of the minds of all socialists.

Profits are divided into two components by economists, "normal profits" and "super-normal profits" or economic rents. While normal profits can possibly be driven down to zero by competition, economic rents never can be, as most market failures except the monopolistic kind are not affected by competition. So bad luck Marxists! Total profits can never be ground down to zero, unless of course the super-normal profits are taxed to zero by a tax on economic rents.

This prevailing belief that economic rents are generally low led to the tacit exclusion of considering taxing any rents except resource rents, when the first effective rent tax in the world was brought in – in Australia. The Petroleum Resource Rent Tax (PRRT) in the early '70s. The PRRT remains very effective though it is not a 'pure' rent tax, as an 'uplift' allowance is used to effectively allow some interest deductions. Subsequently there was an attempt in Australia around 2008 to legislate for a minerals rent tax, but this initiative was completely botched, and failed due to mining industry opposition. However the prevailing and false belief that economic rents are low outside the minerals sector is a major impediment to the introduction of a tax on economic rents. As seen from my previous estimates, non-mining corporate economic rents can be very high.

Economic Rents exist long term – and permanently – and they are a major component of a normal functioning market economy. The reason for this is the very high importance of "market failure" in the economy. Market failure is a permanent and major part of a functioning economy. These market failures are the cause of economic rents, the reason why prices do not fall back to competitive equilibrium – ever.

The study of market failure is becoming central to the study of macroeconomics. It is becoming central to the understanding of how economies work or not work, and why government interventions work or not work. Market failure is the fundamental distinction between micro and macro economics.

So there is no need to use the name "Quasi Rents". Economic Rents are a permanent and important part of any market economy. And they can be taxed.

Chapter 15

Lump Sum Taxes and all that

The lump sum tax

To finish, it might be useful to take a quick trip through lump sum tax land. Taxation economics lecturers usually start with what is considered the most basic possible tax, the lump sum tax, which is a fixed tax which does not vary with anything, and is imposed on the single taxpayer.

As the tax is imposed on a single indivisible person who is unable to evade paying the tax (that is the theory) the supply curve of the tax is vertical. This, as has been previously described, the tax is extremely efficient. It has neither incidence , nor excess burden. The tax cannot be shifted.

BUT the lump sum tax is not *directly* a tax on economic rents. It is therefore distortionary, never the less. The reason is that the tax economics teacher assumes that the taxpayer has sufficient income to pay the tax. If the taxpayer has sufficient income, yes, the tax may be efficient. If there the taxpayer has insufficient income to pay the tax, the tax is not efficient. Simple, but fundamental to taxation economics. At the bottom you are taxing *cash flows*, or trying to.

This is the fundamental reason why taxation on accruals (including some capital gains) is inefficient. You are not taxing cash flows.

The Poll Tax

A vertical supply line does NOT always imply a tax on economic rents. A horrible example is the poll tax or head tax. A Poll Tax is not a tax on economic rents, even if the supply line is vertical. This tax was the nemesis of both Margaret Thatcher and Edward IV of Peasants Revolt fame. "Can't pay, won't pay". To a non-economist it was obvious that the tax was foolish. But to many (badly trained) economists it was an 'ideal tax' because the supply line was vertical, and had no incidence effects.

BUT a poll tax is NOT a tax on economic rents. Why? Because a fixed tax imposed on a person does not mean that the person has any income at all, much less economic rents, to pay the tax. Furthermore, if that person had any economic rents, the poll tax is not related to the size of the economic rents (remember a cash FLOW) earned by that person. The tax was bad economics, and as such idiotic.

To clarify, while taxing economic rents eliminates incidence effects and excess burden, eliminating incidence effects and excess burden does not mean you are taxing economic rents.

Land tax

Yes, a straight tax hit on land values could eliminate incidence effects, but that does not mean that you are taxing economic rents. A lot of rural land, and even some urban land, does not have economic rents.

All things with vertical supply lines do not mean economic rents, and the lack of vertical supply lines does not necessarily mean the lack of economic rents. What is needed is a tax on "unimproved land values" – guaranteed to tax economic rents.

Chapter 16

A Revisionist Theory – The so-called "Modern Theory of Economic Rent"

Now is the time to wrap up this book. But it cannot be closed off without mentioning a new theory of economic rents that has taken possession of the economic profession in certain quarters.

In this new theory, it is argued that the total rent paid is the triangle above the Supply line *abc* in Diagram 13 below. The triangle below the Supply line is called Transfer Earnings. Rent is calculated as the total cost of wages *abcd* less Transfer Earnings *adc*. Transfer earnings mean the amount of money any particular unit could earn in the next best alternative use.

DIAGRAM 13

Modern Theory of Economic Rent

Price

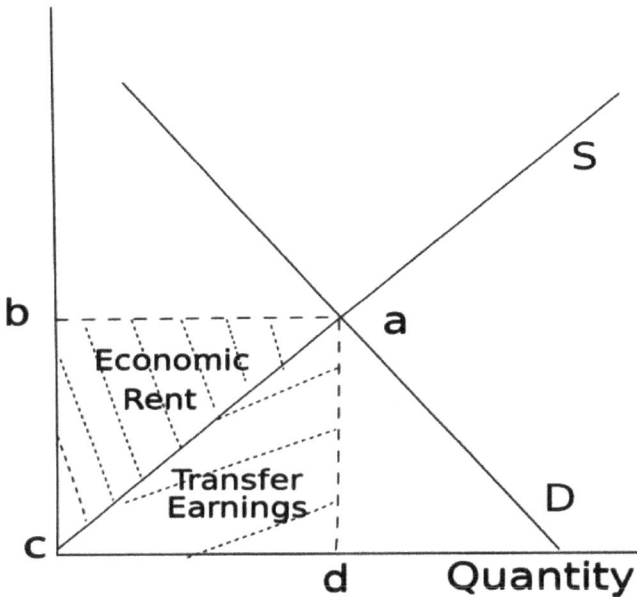

The argument goes like this. "Suppose the diagram is an employment market for nurses. Starting at point *c* and moving towards point *a*, as the wage rate is raised so more nurses are attracted to the profession. At each higher wage, the *new* nurses attracted are getting just enough to persuade them to transfer into the profession. The wage for them is entirely transfer earnings. But nurses already in will get economic rent; after all, they are getting more than necessary to keep them in the profession. Thus at the market wage *b*, the total economic rent of all employed is shown by the area *abc*, the area above the supply curve."[5]

[5] Anonymous person on Pearson Education
http://wps.pearsoned.com.au/wps/media/objects/1634/1674092/case08_5.htm

Now the difference between the two theories is not some minor theoretical issue. If for instance you wanted to estimate the total economic rents in the employed work force, you can either 1. With the Modern Theory of Rent, estimate the supply function for all the job categories, and for each job category estimate the size of the triangle *abc*; or 2. With the Standard Theory of Rent, you calculate the total value of rents from employment by estimating the 'basic wage', *b*, then calculate the difference between the basic wage and the wage of everyone with a wage above *b*, and total them. You would get wildly different answers.

My opinion is that this Modern Theory of Economic Rent is complete nonsense. There are many theoretical objections including the fact that the Modern Theory measure of economic rent coincides with the standard measure of Consumer Surplus and transfer earnings coincide with the standard measure of Producers' Surplus. See the Diagram 14 below and compare it with Diagram 13 above.

DIAGRAM 14

Consumer and Producer Surplus

Price

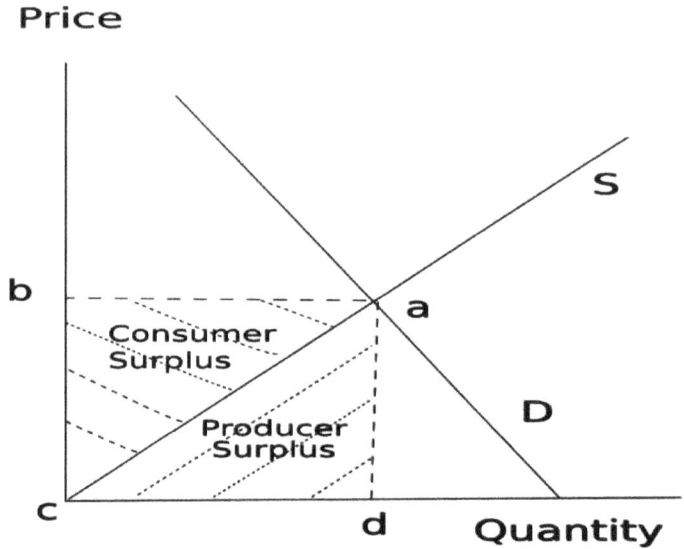

Now producers' surplus certainly cannot be called transfer earnings, because that implies that all the gross profits of the producers end up as wages. Similarly consumer surplus is not rents, as a person with a consumer surplus would not necessarily have any rents in their income.

This 'new theory', I feel, falls down from a logical fallacy, arguing from the particular to the general.

Chapter 17

The value of a Land Tax

One major potential economic rent tax is a tax on land, or more precisely a tax on 'unimproved land values'. In most countries this tax base is neglected, and tax raised from this tax base can be used to replace many inefficient taxes. This chapter provides an example of one such potential replacement. I invite the reader to conduct an exercise on the value of the unimproved land value tax in their own country.

The Goods and Services Tax (GST) is the prevailing sales tax in Australia. Not only is it regressive, but it is highly inefficient. There are significant incidence effects, that is hidden tax transfers, and it has also excess burden rates of around 20 per cent.

On the other hand the land tax is highly efficient. As the tax has a vertical supply curve there are no incidence effects and the excess burden is zero.

A universal land tax, that is a tax on all land in Australia, urban and rural, can very easily replace the GST. It would be very efficient, much more efficient than the GST without the adverse effects of the GST in terms of incidence and excess burden effects.

What is the revenue potential of a universal land tax?

Australian total unimproved land values in 2012 have been estimated by Phillip Soos and Paul Egan (2015) as:

TABLE 11

Residential land	$3,000 billion
Commercial land	$ 351 billion
Rural land	$ 261 billion
Other land markets	$ 225 billion
Total	$4,837 billion

Now a tax of 2% on this is $96 billion.

GST revenue is around $50.5 billion. The budget deficit in 2014-15 was $30 billion.

Thus a 2% land tax could replace the GST and also cover the budget deficit. And as I said it is a far more efficient tax. There would be far lass harm to the economy.

In addition the local government rates could be incorporated into this tax. They could get a cut without having to raise this revenue themselves. It could be argued that this situation could lead to a form of moral hazard. Local governments would spend without having any control or blame about revenue raising. Alternatively their rates could ride on top of that raised by the Federal government. There would be an increase in efficiency in revenue raising.

Wouldn't home-owners scream if they had to pay $4000 or $5000 a year in land tax? But remember they would no longer be paying a 10% GST. While I haven't obtained the distribution of GST payments per level of household income. the lower income households are likely to be net gainers from the abolition of the GST.

Alternatively a much smaller land tax could be used to replace stamp duties. However I feel that there would not be an efficiency gain from this, as stamp duties on land and real property, at least, are already highly efficient. Due to incidence effects, regardless that the buyer nominally pays the tax, the tax actually completely falls on the seller. (It is a tax with a vertical supply line). The buyer would not gain from the abolition of stamp duties, as the price of the property would automatically rise to compensate for the value of the stamp duty. The seller would be the sole gainer from the abolition of stamp duties.

Chapter 18

Mathematical proof that the Brown Tax taxes economic rents

Yes, a mathematical proof is needed. For those whose eyes glaze over, quickly jump this chapter.

I base my proof on the work of the incomparable Robin Boadway, who, over several years spelt out the mathematical basis of taxation and vast areas of public economics. This book is due to his influence, though he always remained disinterested in his academic work and did not stoop to advocate a particular tax.

This proof is a shortened form of his proof on pages 321 to 331 in Boadway and Wildasin (1984).

(a) The no tax case

Suppose the purchase price of one unit of capital is q. The capital is assumed to depreciate proportionately at the rate δ in each period. Then $q\delta$ will be the depreciation incurred during the period on a unit of capital worth q dollars. The cost of financing the asset is assumed to be r dollars per dollar of financing, or qr dollars per unit of capital. The capital loss on the asset will be $-\Delta q$ over the period. The user cost of capital, denoted by c, is the sum of these or:

(20) $c = q(r + \delta + g)$

where $g = \Delta q/q$ is the rate of price change of capital goods.

The firm will invest until the user cost of capital equals the value of the marginal product, or

(21) $p\,MP_k = q(r + \delta - g)$

Where p is the output price, and MP_k is the marginal product of capital.

If the cost of debt is i, cost of equity ρ, B the value of debt, and β he proportion of debt, an $(1 - \beta)$ the proportion of equity, then the cost of finance to the firm will be

(22) $r = Bi + (1 - \beta)\rho$

The no tax case serves as a useful benchmark against which to judge the effect of taxes and inflation. One can think of user cost in Eq. (21) as being the "neutral" user cost of capital. A tax would then be neutral, vis-à-vis the investment decision, if it did not change the expression for the user cost of capital to the firm.

(b) Corporate taxes

To see exactly how the incentive to invest is affected, let the corporate tax rate be u, and let depreciation for tax purposes be at the *declining balance* rate of a. (Other depreciation schedules could also be used). Note that α is not necessarily set equal to the true depreciation rate δ.

Then, as will be explained, the marginal condition satisfied when the firm has chosen its optimal capital stock is

(23) $(1 - u)p\,MP_k = q(r + \delta)\,(1 - u\alpha/(r + \alpha))$

In order to compare this equation with the no tax result Eq. (21), it is useful to rewrite it in the following way:

(24) $p\,MP_k = (q(r + \delta)/(1 - u))(1 - (u\alpha/(r + \alpha)))$

The incentive effect on investment can be obtained by comparing the right-hand side of Eq. (23) with the neutral case $q(r + \delta)$. If the former has been increased by the tax, investment is discouraged, and if decreased by the tax, investment is encouraged. *A priori* it is not obvious whether or not the tax retards or induces investment. It depends on the magnitudes of α and β. In general, however, a tax of this form will not be neutral.

In addition, the tax will distort the choice between debt and equity. By allowing interest deductibility and not equity cost deductibility as well, the tax reduces the relative price of debt financing and induces the firm to increase its debt-equity ratio.

(c) True economic depreciation and full cost of finance deductibility

This is when the actual depreciation rate α equals the true depreciation rate δ, $(\alpha = \delta)$, and both interest costs, i, and equity cost ρ, of holding capital are tax deductible.

The cost of finance, if neither debt nor equity is favoured is:

(25) $r = Bi(1 - u) + (1 - \beta)\rho(1 - u)$

Then Eq (24) can be rewritten :

(26) $pMPk = (q\ (r +\delta)/(1 - u))\ (1 - (\ u\delta/(\ r +\delta)))$

$$= (q\ (r +\delta)/(1 - u))((r + \delta - u\delta)/(r +\delta))$$

$$= q(r +\delta[1 - u])/(1 - u))$$

$$= q(Bi + [1 - \beta]\rho +\delta)$$

as with true economic depreciation and full cost of finance deductibility, the cost of finance of the firm will now be

$r = Bi(1 - u) +(1 - \beta)\rho(1 - u)$

so neither debt nor equity is favoured, as the depreciation rate for tax purposes equals the true depreciation rate, and interest costs, i, and equity costs, ρ, of holding capital are tax deductible.

Equation (26) is the same as the neutral case. This tax scheme, though ideal, is difficult to implement, since the tax authorities must know both the true rate of depreciation, δ, and the imputed cost of finance, ρ. Since neither of these is directly observable, it is unlikely that the tax base could be properly defined.

(d) Writing off capital expenditure when made and interest payments are not deductible (the Brown Tax case)

From here it is a simple step.

First cost of finance becomes

(27) $r = Bi + (1 - \beta)\rho$

since interest is no longer deductible. This is the same as the no tax case of Eq. (22).

Also with immediate write off the depreciation rate α equals ∞.

Eq.(24) can be as:

(28) $p\ MP_k = (q(r + \delta)/(1 - u))(1 - u/((1 + r)/\alpha)$

When $\alpha = \infty$

(29) $p\ MP_k = q(r + \delta)\ (1 - u)/(1 - u)$

This reduces to the no tax case

(30) $p\ MP_k = q(r + \delta)$

This tax is totally neutral with respect to the investment decisions of the firm. It is an ideal, efficient tax, since it collects revenue without imposing any distortions or deadweight loss on the economy.

As Boadway confirms, (Boadway and Wildasin(1984) page 329), on infra-marginal projects, this tax captures the part of the pure profits or rents of a firm. **This tax is a tax on economic rents**.

Chapter 19

Conclusion

A direct tax on economic rents is the only possible non-distortionary tax. It has the advantages of:

1. Business tax revenue will increase substantially immediately, as currently interest deductions (which will be abolished) are far greater than capital expenditure (which can be 100% deducted).

2. Revenue growth will be much faster than under the present system as the economy will be vastly more efficient, as incidence and excess burden costs will be removed.

3. Businesses will invest more compared to the present business tax regime due to 100% deduction of capital expenditure. As capital expenditure carries with it productivity gains, business will become more productive, making the economy more productive, ultimately increasing employment!

4. Estimates are that even with a substantial tax free threshold, there will be a minimal fall in income tax revenue.

5. The economic rent tax is a lot more fair, as only those who can afford to pay tax (have economic rents) will pay tax.

6. The Economic Rent Tax has no Excess Burden. This is a major gain to the economy. This gain can be used to rapidly expand the economy, reducing unemployment.

7. The Economic Rent Tax has no Incidence Effects, or tax shifting in harmful ways. The tax stays with the nominal tax payer. Under the present tax system much of the tax is shifted to the economically weak.

8. Following the two above, the Economic Rent Tax is completely non-distortionary. There are no adverse and costly effects imposed on the economy and individual taxpayers.

9. As a consequence of the higher rate of investment and a non-distortionary tax system, economic growth will be much faster, reducing unemployment.

10. Compliance and collection costs will be much less. Economic rent taxes are far simpler. Furthermore, the arbitrary and nonsensical definitions of profits currently used cause many revenue losses and distortions.

11. The rate of taxes can be increased using the Economic Rent Tax without reducing the incentive to work.

Index

Amit, R. and Paul J. H. Schoemaker. 1993. *"Strategic Assets and Organizational Rent"*, Strategic Management Journal, Vol 14, Issue 1.

Angelson, Karl K., Steinar Olsen. 1987. *"Impact of fish density and effort level on the catching efficiency of fishing gear"*, Fisheries Research, Vol 5, Isssue 2-3, July.

Auerbach, Alan J. and J. R. Hines. 2001, *"Taxation and Economic Efficiency"*, National Bureau of Economic Research, NBER Working Paper 8181.

Ballard, Charles, John Shoven and John Whalley.1985 *"General Equilibrium Computations of the Marginal Welfare Costs of Taxes in the United States"*, American Economic Review 75, pp. 128-138

Ballard, Charles, Don Fullerton. John Shoven and John Whalley. 1985. *"A General Equilibrium Model for Tax Policy Evaluation"*, The University of Chicago Press, Chicago.

Boadway, R.W. and N. Bruce. 1979. *"Depreciation and interest deductions and the effect of the corporation income tax on investment"*, Journal of Public Economics, pp 93-105.

Boadway, R.W. and D. E. Wildasin. 1984. *"Public Sector Economics"* 2nd Edition, Little Brown and Company, Boston.

Chetty, Raj. 2009. "*Is taxable income elasticity sufficient to calculate deadweight loss?*", American Economic Review – Public Policy 1(2):31-52.

Creedy, John. 2003. "*The excess burden of taxation and why it (approximately) quadruples when the tax rate doubles*". New Zealand Treasury Working Paper, 03/29 December 2003.

Creedy, John. 2004. "*The excess burden of taxation*". Australian Economic Review, Vol (37) (4), p 454-464.

Creedy, John. 2009. "*Personal income taxation: from theory to policy*" Australian Economic Review, Vol 42, (4), pp 496-506.

Feldstein, M. 1999 "*Tax Avoidance and the Deadweight Loss of the Income Tax*", Review of Economics and Statistics 81:4, pp. 674-680

Feldstein, M. 2008. "*Effects of Taxation on Economic Behavior*". National Bureau of Economic Research, NBER Working Paper 13754.

Harberger, A. 1971. "*Three Basic Postulates for Applied Welfare Economics: an Interpretive Essay*", Journal of Economic Literature, 9, pp. 785-97.

Hausman, J. '*Labor Supply*' in H. Aaron and J. Pechman (eds). 1981. "*How Taxes Affect Economic Behaviour* ", (Washington D.C.: The Brookings Institution)

George, Henry. 1879, *"Progress and Poverty"*.

Nitzan, Shmuel. 1994 *"Modelling Rent Seeking Contests"*, European Journal of Political Economy, vol 10, Issue 1, May, pp 41-60.

Prest, A.R. 1981. *"The Taxation of Urban Land"*, Manchester University Press.

Ricardo, David. 1817. *"Principles of Political Economy and Taxation"*.

Robson, A. 2005. *"The Cost of Taxation"*, Centre of Independent Studies, CIS Policy Monograph 68, Page 7.

Soos, Phillip and Paul Egan. 2015. *"Bubble Economics: Australian Land Speculation 1830-2013"*, Book available on the internet.

Wanniski, J. 1978. *"Taxes, Revenue and the Laffer Curve"*, The Public Interest, No 50, Winter, pp. 3-16.

Yorgenson D. and K. Yun. 1990 *"Tax Reform and Economic Growth"*, Journal of Political Economy, 98:5, pp. 151-93

Yorgenson, D. and K. Yun. 1991 *"The Excess Burden of Taxation in the United States"*, Journal of Accounting and Finance 6:4, pp 487-50.

www.ingramcontent.com/pod-product-compliance
Lightning Source LLC
Chambersburg PA
CBHW060633210326
41520CB00010B/1591